C. A White

The Student's Mythology

A Compendium of Greek, Roman, Egyptian, Assyrian, Persian, Hindoo...

C. A White

The Student's Mythology
A Compendium of Greek, Roman, Egyptian, Assyrian, Persian, Hindoo...

ISBN/EAN: 9783337008550

Printed in Europe, USA, Canada, Australia, Japan

Cover: Foto ©ninafisch / pixelio.de

More available books at **www.hansebooks.com**

THE
STUDENT'S MYTHOLOGY

A COMPENDIUM

OF

Greek, Roman, Egyptian, Assyrian, Persian, Hindoo, Chine
Thibetian, Scandinavian, Celtic, Aztec, and Peruvian
Mythologies,

IN ACCORDANCE WITH STANDARD AUTHORITIES.

ARRANGED FOR THE USE OF SCHOOLS AND
ACADEMIES.

BY

C. A. WHITE.

NEW EDITION, REVISED AND CORRECTED.

NEW YORK.
A. C. ARMSTRONG & SON,
714 BROADWAY.
1889.

Entered According to Act of Congress in the year 1870, by
W. J. WIDDLETON,
In the Clerk's Office of the District Court of the United States for
the Southern District of New York.
Copyright, 1882, by W. C. Bush.

PREFATORY NOTE.

The Student's Mythology has been in use in manuscript for nearly three years in one of our largest academies, where it has been received with much favor by both teachers and pupils. Even in that form, which subjected them to the inconvenience of long dictations, it was preferred to any of the ordinary text-books on the subject. Copies were sought for the use of other institutions, and the principals of the academy referred to, consented that the work should be prepared for the press.

In carrying out the plan, the subject matter was carefully classified, and such additions made as were deemed necessary for completeness. As a farther precaution, the whole was submitted to the revision of an eminent classical scholar.

Irish Chroniclers and other standard authorities. The matter of the Mexican and Peruvian mythologies, has been chiefly taken from Clavigero and Prescott. Reference has been made throughout to the New American Cyclopædia.

The work now completed is offered to the public in the hope that it may render the subject of mythology more generally popular in our schools, and obviate the dangers attending this otherwise attractive study.

CONTENTS.

CHAPTER I.

Origin of Mythology—Divinities called Celestial. 21

CHAPTER II.

Greek and Roman Divinities—Jupiter—Juno—How represented—Parentage and Actions—Probable Origin of these Fables—Adventures of Jupiter—Story of Europa—Search of Cadmus—Punishment of Lycaon 23

CHAPTER III.

Apollo—His Parentage and Exploits—How represented—Story of Æsculapius—Banishment of Apollo from Heaven—Transformation of Hyacinthus and Cyparissus—Story of Admetus and Alcestis—Attributes of Apollo—Punishment inflicted on Marsyas and on King Midas—Story of Midas—Death of Phæton—Transformation of Daphne—Things Sacred to Apollo 29

CHAPTER IV.

Mars (Ares)—His Parentage—How represented—Animals Sacred to Mars—Names given to Mars—His Temple—Priests called Salii. . 34

CHAPTER V.

Mercury (Hermes)—His Parentage—How represented—Offices of Mercury—Benefits conferred by Mercury on Man—Why considered the Patron of Thieves—Story of Io and Argus. 36

CHAPTER VI.

Bacchus (Dionysus)—Parentage of the God—How represented—Story of Semele—Infancy of Bacchus—Transformation of Nymphs into

Stars—Silenus—How represented—Exploits of Bacchus—How worshipped—Plants Sacred to the God—Bacchanalia or Orgia—Story of Pentheus—Punishment inflicted on Alcithoe and her Sisters—Transformation of Mariners into Dolphins. 33

CHAPTER VII.

Celestial Goddesses— Juno—Hera—Parentage of Juno—How represented —Iris, Messenger of Juno—Children of Juno—Jealousy of the Goddess—Transformation of Callista and Arcas into Bears—Sacrifices offered to the Goddess—Plants held Sacred to her. 43

CHAPTER VIII.

Minerva—Pallas Athena—How represented—Origin of the Olive—The Palladium—Minerva, as the Patroness of Female Industry—Story of Arachne—The Bird of Minerva—Story of Medusa's Head. . 45

CHAPTER IX.

Venus—Aphrodite—Birth and Education of Venus—Marriage with Vulcan—How represented—Temples of Venus—The Graces—Cupid—Festivals of the Goddess—Birds and Plants Sacred to her—Sacrifices—Temple of Venus Calva—The Apple of Discord—Decision of Paris—Story of Hippomenes and Atalanta—Death of Adonis—Origin of the Red Rose—Names of the Graces. . . 49

CHAPTER X.

Latona—Leto—Her Parentage—Persecution of Juno—Birth of Apollo and Diana—Transformation of Lycian Peasants into Frogs—Punishment of Tityus—Latona a Personification of Night—How represented by Painters and Sculptors. 51

CHAPTER XI.

Aurora—Eos—Attributes of the Goddess—How represented—Story of Cephalus and Procris—Marriage of Aurora with Tithonus—Transformation of Tithonus—Memnon—His Death and Obsequies—Vocal Statue. 54

CHAPTER XII.

Terrestrial Gods—Saturn—His Parentage—How represented—His History—The Golden Age—Sacrifices offered to Saturn—The Saturnalia —Modern Carnival—Janus—Contradictory Accounts of his Origin—Temple of Janus—Quirinus at Rome. . . . . . .

Contents.

CHAPTER XIII.

Vulcan—Hephæstus—Parentage of this God—Why banished from Heaven—Occupation of Vulcan—His Most Celebrated Works—Marriage with Venus—The Cyclops—Vulcania—Temple on Mount Etna—Cacus—Cœculus—Other Works of Vulcan. . . . 64

CHAPTER XIV.

Æolus—Supposed origin of the Fable-Minus—His Parentage—Criticisms passed on other Divinities—His Banishment from Olympus 67

CHAPTER XV.

Terrestrial Goddesses—Vesta—Hestia—Her Parentage and Attributes—How represented—Worship of Vesta at Rome—Vestal Virgins—Their Obligations and Privileges—Anecdote. 69

CHAPTER XVI.

Cybele—How called by the Greeks—Parentage and Attributes—How represented—Temple of Cybele on Mount Dindymus—Sacred Image—Festival of Megalecia—Galle and Corybantes—Bona Dea—Story of the Vestal Claudia. 72

CHAPTER XVII.

Ceres—Demeter—Parentage and Attributes—How represented—Story of Proserpine—Eleusinian Mysteries—Rites practiced—Story of Triptolemus—Sacrifices offered to Ceres—Feasts called Ambarvalia—Described by Virgil. . . . . . , , . . 75

CHAPTER XVIII.

Themis—Origin and Attributes—Astræa changed into the Constellation Virgo—Erigone—Nemesis—Her Office—Temp'e of Nemesis at Rhamnus. 80

CHAPTER XIX.

The Muses—Their Number, Names and Attributes—Why there are Nine Muses—Punishment of the Daughters of Pierus. . . . 82

CHAPTER XX.

Gods of the Woods, and Rural Deities—Pan—Names given to this Deity—His Origin—How represented—Famous Action related of Pan—Origin of Pan's Reeds—Satyrs and Fauns—Terminus—Vertumnus—Pales. 84

CHAPTER XXI.

Goddesses of the Woods—Diana—Parentage and Attributes of this Goddess—How represented—Habits of Diana—Her Attendants—Punishment of Chione—Story of Niobe—Temple of Diana at Ephesus—Burned by Erostratus—Despoiled by Nero—Plundered by the Goths—Nymphs—Naiades—Oreades—Oceanides—Dryades and Hamadryades—Arethusa—Story of Echo—Transformation of Narcissus. 81

CHAPTER XXII.

Gods of the Sea—Neptune—Poseidon—Parentage of the God—How represented—Offices of Neptune—Feasts held at Rome in his Honor—Children of Neptune—Triton—Phorcus or Proteus—Sirens—Ulysses—Orpheus—Scylla and Charybdis—Melicertes—Thetis—Glaucus 93

CHAPTER XXIII.

Infernal Deities—Pluto—Hades—Parentage of the God—His Kingdom—Representations and Emblems—Dis—Plutus—Hell—Cerberus—Fates—Furies—Judges of the Dead—Punishment inflicted on the Condemned—Giants—Ixion—Sisyphus—Tantalus—The Belides—Salmoneus—Elysium 99

CHAPTER XXIV.

Fabulous Monsters—Centaurs—Geryon—Harpies—Briareus—The Chimæra—Explanation of this Fable—The Sphinx—Fabulous History—Statue of the Sphinx in Egypt. 105

CHAPTER XXV.

Household Divinities—Penates—Offices and Attributes—Lares—Their Offices—Sacrifices offered to the Goddess Mania—Honors paid to the Lares—Virtues worshipped as Divinities. 108

CHAPTER XXVI.

Demigods and Heroes—Their Origin—Hercules—His Parentage—Twelve Labors of the Hero—Field of Narbonne—Death of Hercules. 114

CHAPTER XXVII.

Jason—Expedition in search of the Golden Fleece—Medea—Her Revenge—Theseus—Tribute imposed on the Athenians—Departure of Theseus—Destruction of the Minotaur—Ariadne—Death of Ægeus. 119

CONTENTS.

CHAPTER XXVIII.

Castor and Pollux—Their Parentage—Death of Castor—Constellation Gemini—Prometheus—His Parentage—His Impiety—Pandora's Box—Punishment of Prometheus 118

CHAPTER XXIX.

Orpheus—Story of Eurydice—Death of Orpheus—Transformation of Thracian Women into Trees—Arion—Amphion. 124

CHAPTER XXX.

Atlas—His Parentage—Transformed by Perseus into a Mountain—Explanation of the Fable—Pleiades—Hyades—Hesperides—Orion—His Parentage, Exploits and Death—Transformation into a Constellation—Perseus—His Parentage—Rescue of Andromeda—Death of Acrisius 128

CHAPTER XXXI.

Bellerophon—Victory over the Chimæra—His Presumption and its Punishment—Deucalion—Legend of the re-peopling of the Earth after the Deluge—Probable Explanation—Dædalus—Labyrinth—Death of Icarus—Ceyx—Alcyone—Halcyon Birds. . . . 134

CHAPTER XXXII.

Meleager—The Calydonian Hunt—Erisichthon, Nisus and Scylla. . 140

CHAPTER XXXIII.

Poets of Classic Fable—Homer—Hesiod—Virgil—Ovid. . . . 145

CHAPTER XXXIV.

Heroes Celebrated by the Poets—Agamemnon—Sacrifice of Iphigenia—Quarrel with Achilles—Murder of Agamemnon by Ægisthus and Clytemnestra—Achilles—His Parentage—Discovered by Ulysses at the Court of Lycomedes—His Quarrel with Agamemnon—Death of Patroclus—Exploits during the Siege—Death of Achilles—Sacrifice of Polyxena—Transformation of Hecuba. 152

CHAPTER XXXV.

Ulysses—His Marriage with Penelope—Feigned Insanity—Exploits during the Siege of Troy—Lotus Eaters—Slaying of the Sacred Cattle by the Sailors—Their destruction—Ulysses in the Island of Calypso—Cast on the Shores of Phæacia—His Arrival in Ithaca—Suitors of Penelope—Her Deliverance by Ulysses. 159

CHAPTER XXXVI.

Orestes—Education at the Court of Strophius—Pylades—Murder of Clytemnestra—Orestes pursued by the Furies—Discovery of Iphigenia at Tauris—Circumstances added by the Tragic Poets—Hector—Character and Exploits of the Hero; his Death—Fate of Astyanax—Œdipus—Eteocles and Polynices—Theban War—Heroism of Antigone. 164

CHAPTER XXXVII.

Æneas—His Parentage—His Flight from Troy—Interview with Andromache at Epirus—Prophecy of Helenus—Æneas driven by a Storm on the Coast of Africa—Received by Dido at Carthage—Departure of Æneas—Death of Dido—Funeral Games—Descent into the Infernal Regions—Landing of Æneas in Italy—War—Death of Turnus and Marriage of Æneas with Lavinia—His Death. . 171

CHAPTER XXXVIII.

Sibyls—Story of the Cumæan Sibyl—Legend of the Sibylline Books—Their destruction—Opinions entertained regarding these Verses—Divination by Omens—The Augurs—Different Classes of Omens—Anecdote. 176

CHAPTER XXXIX.

Oracles—Oracle of Jupiter at Dodona—Manner of giving Responses—Oracle of Delphi—Account given by Diodorus—The Pythia—Remarkable Responses—Unsuccessful attempts made to plunder this Temple—Despoiled by Nero and others—Oracle of Trophonius—Story of the Hero and his Brother—Agamedes—Discovery of the Oracle—Peculiar Rites observed by the Votaries—Oracle of Jupiter Ammon—Its Situation—Temple founded by Bacchus—Expedition sent by Cambyses—Ruins still existing—Fons Solis—Account given by Belzoni—Oracle of Esculapius at Epidaurus—Remarkable Embassy sent to Epidaurus by the Roman Senate—Treatment of Votaries in the different Oracles of Esculapius—Oracle of the Castalian Fount—Anecdote of the Emperor Hadrian—Opinions entertained with regard to these Oracles—Quotation from Milton. . 180

CHAPTER XL.

Classic Games—Why connected with Mythology—Olympic Games—By Whom instituted—Time and Manner of their celebration—Olym-

Contents. 11

Pads -Nature of the Contests—Qualifications required of the Competitors—Prize awarded to the Victors—Honors bestowed—Horse and Chariot Races—Philip of Macedon—Alcibiades—Cynisca—Intellectual Contests—Herodotus—Dionysius—Pythian Games—By whom instituted—Time of their Celebration—Prize—Nemean Games—Crowns bestowed—Isthmian Games—Why so called—Instituted in Honor of Melicertes—Garland bestowed on the Victor. . 181

CHAPTER XLI.

The Greek Drama—Peculiarities of the Greek Theatre—Description of the Theatre of Bacchus at Athens—Stage Machinery—Dress of the Actors—Masks—The Chorus—Measures of the Choral Dance—Chorus of the Furies—Story of Ibycus—Attempt made to revive the Ancient Chorus—Time occupied by Theatrical Entertainments—Their cost—Comparison with the Roman Amphitheatre. . . 197

CHAPTER XLII.

Celebrated Statues—The Olympian Jupiter—Minerva of the Parthenon—Subsequent Fate of this Temple—Apollo Belvidere—Diana à la Biche 206

PART II.

CHAPTER I.

Egyptian Divinities—Osiris—Apis and Serapis—Parentage of Osiris—His Death and Sepulture—Isis—Attributes—Emblematic representation—Rites of Isis forbidden at Rome—Condemned by Juvenal—Apis—Manner of transmigration—Festivals in Honor of Apis—Discovery of a Successor—Oracles obtained from this Divinity—Germanicus—Harpocrates—Quotation 208

CHAPTER II.

Eastern Mythology—Divinities of the Assyrians—Baal or Bel—Tower of Babel—Proper Names of the Phœnicians and Carthaginians—Worship of Baal introduced among the Israelites by Achab—Reproaches of Jeremias—Moloch—Nations devoted to his Worship—Human Sacrifices—Representation of this God—His Worship forbidden by Moses—Valley of Hinnom—Quotation from Milton—Ashtaroth or Astarte—Sacrifices in Honor of this Goddess—Abuses attending her Festivals—Thammuz identical with Adonis—Mourned by the Assyrian Women—Lines from Milton—Vision of Ezekiel—Oannes—Dagon 213

CHAPTER III.

Persia—The Zend-avesta—Doctrines of Zoroaster—Ormuzd or Orinasdes—Ahriman—Worship of Fire—The Guebers—Perpetual Fires—Bakoo—Magic and Astrology—Parsees of Hindostan. . . . 218

CHAPTER IV.

Hindoo Mythology—Brahma—The Vedas—Doctrine of the Vedas—Brahma, Vishnu and Siva—Offices of these Deities—Avatars of Vishnu—Krishna—Siva—Doctrines regarding the Soul—Metempsychosis—Castes—Buddha—His Doctrines—Buddhism suppressed in India 222

CHAPTER V.

China—Absence of any State Religion in China—Doctrine of the Lettered—Confucius—His Writings—Honors paid him in China—Difficulties occasioned among Christian Missionaries—Lao-tze, founder of the Religion of Tao or Reason—His Writings—Chinese Buddhists—Temple of Buddha at Pou-tou—General Feeling of the Chinese with regard to Religion. 229

CHAPTER VI.

Thibet—The Grand Lama—Prevailing Religion of Thibet and Tartary—Lamaseries—The Grand Lama, a Perpetual Incarnation of Buddha—His transmigrations—Mode of discovering his Successor 236

CHAPTER VII.

Mythology of Scandinavia—Compared with that of Greece and Rome—The Eddas—Account of the Creation—Form of the Earth—Asgard, Odin—Names of this Deity—Valhalla—Thor—Recovery of Thor's Hammer—Frey and Freya—Bragi—Heimdall—Vidar—Hodur—The Valkyrior—Loki and his Progeny—Death of Baldur—His Funeral—Loki's Punishment—The Elves—Runic Letters—Ragnarok, the Twilight of the Gods. 238

CHAPTER VIII.

Celtic Mythology—Druidism—Derivation of the Word Druid—Origin of Druidical Worship—Account given by Cæsar—Characteristics Divinities worshipped by the Druids—Esus—His Attributes—Bel—Teutates—Camul—Tarann—Priests—Their Duties—Bards—Their Influences—Druids, properly so called—Sacred Plants—Mystic Writing of the Druids—Their Political Authority—Druidesses—Of the Loire—Of the Island of Sena—Human Sacrifices offered by Druidesses—Virgins of Tara—Sacrifices offered by the Druids—Victims chosen—Belief of the Druids in a Future State—Festivals

CONTENTS.

of the Druids—Festival—Solstices—Beltane or Bealtime—Ceremonies observed in Ireland—St. Patrick at Tara—First of November—Breton Legend—Superstitious Practices belonging to the Day—Suppression of Druidism in Gaul—In England—Mona—Iona—Druidical Monuments—Menhirs—Dolmens—Cromlechs—Stonehenge—Carnac—Popular Superstitions 251

CHAPTER IX.

Mexico—Mythology of the Aztecs—Its Peculiar Characteristics—Belief of the Aztecs with regard to the Supreme Being—Subordinate Deities—Huitzilopotchli—Legend of Quetzalcoatl—Household Divinities—Belief of the Aztecs with regard to a Future State—Singular Ceremony—Rites of Burial—Aztec Priests—Priestesses—Mexican Temples—Pyramid of Cholula—Sacrifices—Their Number—Victims offered annually to Tetzcatlipoca—Cannibal Repasts—Montezuma 274

CHAPTER X.

Mythology of the Ancient Peruvians—Belief in One God—Worship of the Sun—Moon, and Stars—Legend of Manco-Capac—Pretended Origin of the Inca Race—Legend of the Deluge—Tradition of White Men from the East—Temple of the Sun in the Island of Titicaca—Temple of Cuzco—Peruvian Priesthood—Sacrifices offered to the Sun—Festivals of the Sun—Feast of Raymi—Resemblance of certain Peruvian Rites to those observed by the Ancient Romans—Virgins of the Sun—Burial Rites of the Peruvians—Cupay 284

SUPPLEMENT.

Notice of Authors, etc., mentioned in this Volume—Æschylus—Cæsar—Cicero—Demosthenes—Diodorus—Euripides—Herodotus—Justin—Juvenal—Mæcenas—Pelasgi—Plinius—Procopius—Simonides—Sophocles—Strabo—Titicaca—Varro . . . . . .

MYTHOLOGY.

CHAPTER I.

Ques. What is Mythology?

Ans. This word is derived from the Greek, *Mythos*, a myth or fable, and *logos*, a discourse. A myth is, properly speaking, an allegory or fable invented to convey some important moral or religious truth, or illustrate some operation of nature. Mythology includes also the historical myths, or the narratives of gods, demigods, and heroes, which were current among the heathen in ancient times.

Ques. Why is it necessary to become acquainted with these fables?

Ans. Because ancient literature and art cannot be fully understood or appreciated without some knowledge of Mythology. It was mingled with every theme of the classic poet, and inspired the highest skill of the painter and sculptor.

These subjects keep their place to some extent in modern art, and mythological allusions are so frequent in our literature that an acquaintance with classic fable is considered a necessary part of a liberal education.

Ques. Did all the heathen nations worship the same deities?

Ans. The mythology of different nations varied as to the names and attributes of their divinities. There are, nevertheless, so many points of resemblance, that it is believed by many that the principal mythical systems had one common origin. To trace these analogies, and the developments which gave rise to so great a diversity, is the province of comparative mythology.

Ques. In what important point do all these systems agree?

Ans. In the rite of sacrifice. We meet everywhere the same offerings: flowers, first fruits, libations of milk, honey, and wine; also sacrifices of animals, which were either partaken of by the votaries or consumed as holocausts upon the altar.

This mode of worship varied but little in ceremonial, and the sacrifices of the different heathen nations resembled, in their exterior form, those offered to the true God by the ancient patriarchs. The idea of propitiating the deity in such a manner seems to have been universal both in the old and the new world, and we are forced to believe that it was drawn from a common fount of primeval tradition.

Ques. How did the belief in the heathen deities originate?

Ans. When the early traditions of the human race became corrupt, the sublime idea of one God, self-existent and eternal, was lost or obscured. We find it, though vaguely perhaps, in the character and attributes of certain divinities, as the Zeus (Jupiter) of the Greek, and the Alfâdur of Scandinavian mythology. There are passages in the early Greek poets which show clearly a belief in the unity of God. In the verses attributed to the mythic poet Orpheus, and generally known as Orphic Remains, we find the following:

"One self-existent lives; created things
Arise from him; and He is all in all.
No mortal sight may see Him, yet Himself
Sees all that live; * * *
 * * * For He alone
All heavenly is, and all terrestrial things
Are wrought by Him. First, midst and last he holds
With His omniscient grasp."

The same idea is expressed in the verses of the poet Aratus, quoted by St. Paul in his address to the Athenians on the Hill of Mars.

Instead of ministering spirits obeying the will

of the Supreme Being, and communicating that will to man, there arose a number of inferior deities, each exercising some peculiar and partial sovereignty. The god whom the warrior invoked in battle was powerless to bless the field he cultivated in time of peace; the power of Jupiter was worshipped in the rolling thunder; but when the earth trembled or fiery torrents burst from the mountain top, the wrath of Pluto must be appeased, and sacrifices were offered to the infernal powers. The strife and turbulence of nature were attributed to the gods, who became in some manner identified with the elements they were supposed to govern.

The honors paid to the memory of departed heroes assumed, in the course of time, the character of religious worship. Hence arose a class of demigods, whose real achievements, transmitted by popular tradition and embellished by the poets, became altogether legendary and mythical.

Ques. Were the Greek and Roman mythologies the same?

Ans. They were, to a great extent. The ancient Latins had, undoubtedly, their own gods and their peculiar superstitions, but they do not appear to have had any regular mythology. When the Romans received the arts and sciences from the Greeks, they adopted, also, their divinities and their entire system of religion.

Ans. They shared a tradition, which seems to have been universal, of a time of primeval innocence, when man dwelt in a peaceful world, ignorant alike of sorrow and of sin. This was the Golden Age. Avarice and discord were unknown; men had not learned to slay animals for food, nor had the earth been disturbed by the plough. Neither the labors of the husbandman, nor the merchant's traffic disturbed the joyous leisure of that happy time; no ships ploughed the seas, and the glittering steel rested harmless in the mine. Ovid thus describes the days of innocence:

> "The Golden Age was first, when man, yet new,
> No rule but uncorrupted reason knew,
> And, with a native bent did good pursue.
> Unforced by punishment, unawed by fear,
> His words were simple, and his soul sincere ;
> Needless was written law where none oppressed ;
> The law of man was written in his breast :
> No suppliant crowds before the judge appeared,
> No court erected yet, nor cause was heard,
> But all was safe ; for conscience was their guard.
> * * * * * * *
> No walls were yet, nor fence, nor moat, nor mound,
> Nor drum was heard, nor trumpet's angry sound,
> Nor swords were forged ; but, void of care and crime,
> The soft creation slept away their time."

The Silver Age was far inferior to that of gold; but virtue still dwelt on earth, and the Immortals had not altogether departed from the abodes of men. Jupiter then divided the year into seasons, shortened the winter days, and let loose the northern blasts, so that men were obliged to build dwellings, and cultivate the ungrateful soil.

Their first habitations were caves and grottoes, leafy coverts of the forest, or huts rudely constructed of the trunks of trees and interwoven boughs.

The Brazen Age came next; men grew fierce and warlike, but were not as yet altogether impious.

The Iron Age gave birth to all the calamities that afflict mankind. Avarice and violence reigned supreme; men were not satisfied to till the earth, but dug into its hidden mines, and drew thence gold and iron, potent instruments of ill to man.

The same poet says:

> "Then land-marks limited to each his right;
> For all before was common as the light.
> Nor was the ground alone required to bear
> Her annual income to the crooked share,
> But greedy mortals, rummaging her store,
> Digged from her entrails first the precious ore
> (Which next to hell the prudent gods had laid,)
> And that alluring ill to sight displayed.
> Thus cursed steel, and more accursed gold,
> Gave mischief birth, and made that mischief bold
> And double death did wretched man invade,
> By steel assaulted, and by gold betrayed."
>
> *Dryden's Ovid.*

MOUNT OLYMPUS.

Ques. Where were the gods supposed to dwell?

Ans. On the summit of Mount Olympus, in Thessaly. This mountain hides its head, covered with perpetual snows, in a belt of clouds. The

Greeks imagined above these, a sublime abode reposing in eternal sunshine, and free from the storms which vexed the lower world. A gate of clouds, guarded by the goddesses of the seasons, opened to permit the passage of the Celestials when they descended to earth. Each god had his own dwelling, but all were obliged to repair, when summoned, to the palace of Jupiter. Even those deities whose usual abode was on the earth, in the waters, or in the lower shades, were compelled to assemble in Olympus at his command. Here they feasted on ambrosia and nectar, discoursed upon the affairs of heaven and earth, and were delighted at intervals by the music of Apollo's lyre, and the songs of the Muses.

Vulcan was smith, architect and chariot builder to the gods. He built their dwellings on Olympus, and constructed the furniture in so wonderful a manner, that the tripods and tables were endowed with motion, and ranged themselves in order without the aid of hands. The robes of the different divinities were wrought by Minerva and the Graces. Everything of a solid nature was constructed of metal.

THE GODS—DIFFERENT CLASSES OF DEITIES.

Ques. Did the Greeks believe that the gods resembled men?

Ans. Yes; in many particulars. They supposed them to have the same passions, both good and evil. They were immortal, yet could suffer pain and receive wounds. Instead of blood a fluid called ichor filled their veins. The deities resembled men also in form, but they were, with some exceptions, of majestic stature and shone with celestial beauty. They could render themselves invisible at will, and were otherwise endowed with supernatural powers. There was this restraint upon their wonder-working gifts: no divinity was permitted to reverse the act of another. For example, when an offended god subjected a mortal to some cruel transformation, no other deity, not even Jupiter himself, could undo the spell.

Ques. Into what classes were the gods divided?

Ans. Ancient writers differ in the classification of the Greek and Roman divinities. According to one division, which we will follow, the Celestial gods were: Jupiter, Apollo, Mars, Mercury and Bacchus. The goddesses were: Juno, Minerva or Pallas, Venus, Aurora and Latona.

To these higher divinities, Saturn, Janus, Vesta and others were sometimes added. There were also Terrestrial divinities, Gods of the Sea, Infernal deities, etc. etc.

CHAPTER II.

GREEK AND ROMAN DIVINITIES

Celestial Gods.

JUPITER, (Greek, *Zeus.*)

Ques. Who was Jupiter?

Ans. He was the king and father of gods and men. He is generally represented as a majestic man with a beard, sitting on a throne of gold and ivory. He brandishes the thunder in his right hand; giants lie prostrate under his feet, and an eagle stands at his side. Jupiter is sometimes called Jove, and as the eagle was sacred to him, it is often called the bird of Jove.

Ques. Relate the story of Diony'sius and Jupiter's cloak.

Ans. The statues of this god were sometimes decorated with much magnificence. It is related that Diony'sius, the tyrant of Syracuse, visited a temple in Sicily, where he saw a statue of Jupiter arrayed in a mantle of wrought gold. This he took possession of, and ordered in its place a woolen cloak. Diony'sius justified the act on the plea that the latter garment would be more comfortable for the god at all seasons, as it was neither so heavy in summer, nor so cold in winter.

Ques. Of whom was Jupiter the son?

Ans. He was the son of Saturn and Ops. According to the fable, Saturn promised his brother Titan, that after his death, the latter should succeed him in his kingdom. To ensure this, Titan made Saturn promise farther to destroy all his male children. In fulfillment of this engagement, Saturn devoured them as soon as they were born. Ops, or Rhea, his wife, succeeded in concealing Jupiter from him. She sent him secretly to Crete where he was educated on Mount Ida, by the nymphs, or, according to some, by the priestesses of Cyb'ele. The goat which suckled him was placed afterwards amongst the constellations. Ops saved Neptune and Pluto in the same manner.

Ques. What were Jupiter's first exploits?

Ans. Titan was so much enraged against Saturn for failing to destroy all his male children, that he assembled the giants, generally called Titans, to avenge the injury. They overcame Saturn, and bound him with Ops, or Rhea, in hell. Jupiter conquered the Titans, and delivered his father and mother. He afterwards took up arms against Saturn himself, whom he overcame and banished. He then shared his power with his two brothers, Neptune and Pluto; to Neptune he gave the command of the seas and rivers, while Pluto received for his portion the subterranean world, or infernal regions.

Ques. What natural phenomena were attributed to Jupiter?

Ans. Thunder, lightning, rain, clouds, snow, and rainbows. These were sent by Jupiter either as signs or warnings, or else to punish the transgressions of men, particularly the perversion of law and justice. It seems certain that the ancients regarded Jupiter as a righteous power, the enemy of tyrants, and the protector of the poor and innocent. It is hard to reconcile this character with the fables which ascribe to this god actions in the last degree base and criminal.

Ques. How would you explain this seeming contradiction?

Ans. Many of these stories were simply allegories, illustrating the dominion of Jupiter over the natural world. Others were invented at later times; and all were embellished by the poets with but little regard for moral or religious sentiment. Whatever their origin, there can be no doubt that they had an unfavorable influence on the pagan world, and that they contributed to weaken whatever respect remained for public or private virtue.

Ques. Relate some of these fables?

Ans. Jupiter was married to Juno, to whom he first appeared in the form of a crow. He constantly excited her jealousy by his admiration of mortal women, and this gave rise to many adventures, celebrated by the poets.

Ques. What was the story of Euro′pa?

Ans. Jupiter was struck by the beauty of Euro'pa, daughter of Age'nor, king of Phœnicia. He took the form of a snow-white bull, and mingled with the herd that grazed in the meadow where the young princess was gathering flowers. Euro'pa, attracted by the beauty and gentleness of the animal, caressed him, crowned him with flowers, and at length fearlessly mounted on his oack. He immediately plunged into the sea, and carried her to the unknown shores of Europe, which was named from her.

Ques. On what was the story of Euro'pa probably founded?

Ans. It is probable that some sea captain, or pirate, was attracted by the beauty of the young princess, and carried her off. When her father grieved at her loss, the courtiers, and perhaps the oracles, pretended that it was a god who had taken her away. As this report was flattering to his pride, he would of course be pleased to hear it everywhere repeated. This, however, did not prevent Age'nor from making every effort to recover his lost child.

Ques. Relate the story of Cadmus.

Ans. Cadmus, the son of Age'nor, was ordered by his father to go in search of his sister Euro'pa, with the further injunction, that he should never return to his native land without her. The search proved fruitless, and Cadmus, not daring to appear before his father, went to consult the oracle of Apollo as to what he should do. He was directed by the god to follow a young heifer, which he would meet in the fields, and to mark the place where she should lie down to rest. He was to build a city on that spot, and call the surrounding country Bœotia. Cadmus obeyed these instructions; while preparing to offer sacrifice to Jupiter on the site of his intended town, the solemnity was interrupted by a terrible event. The attendants of Cadmus, in searching for water, had entered a grove sacred to Mars, which was guarded by a mighty dragon. On perceiving him, they turned to fly, but were either crushed in the serpent's folds, or suffocated by blasts of the monster's fiery breath. Cadmus, awaiting their return, and becoming impatient at the delay, proceeded to the spot, and found his servants lifeless, while the dragon was basking at his ease upon the grass. The hero, aroused to vengeance, attacked the monster. A terrible combat ensued, in which Cadmus, through the assistance of Minerva, was victorious. As he gazed upon his expiring foe, he heard a frightful voice which threatened him with the vengeance of the god whose grove he had desecrated. Cadmus was at first dismayed, but Minerva told him to sow the dragon's teeth in the ground, and await the result. Where the teeth were planted, armed men immediately sprung up. Cadmus threw a stone among them, upon which they turned their weapons against one another, and continued to fight until all were killed except five. These assisted the hero in building his city.

Cadmus married Hermi'one, the daughter of Venus; they had four daughters, all of whom suffered persecution, either in their own persons, or in those of their children. Cadmus and Hermi'one were so much afflicted by the misfortunes of their descendants, that they petitioned the gods to deprive them of life. They were soon after changed into serpents.

Ques. Relate the punishment of Lyca'on.

Ans. During the Iron Age the wickedness of men had grown to such a height that Jupiter resolved to satisfy himself of the truth of the reports that reached him. For this purpose he descended to earth, and assuming the disguise of a poor traveller, sought hospitality of Lyca'on, king of Arcadia. The impious prince had just received an ambassador from the Molossians. He ordered him to be slain, and his flesh to be served for the entertainment of his guest. Jupiter was seized with indignation; he overturned the tables, destroyed the palace with lightning; and when the tyrant strove to fly, he was transformed into a savage wolf.

CHAPTER III.

PHŒBUS—APOLLO.

Ques. Who was Apollo?

Ans. He was the son of Jupiter and Lato'na. This god was, with his twin-sister Diana, born at Delos, an island in which Lato'na had taken refuge from the anger of Juno. This goddess, jealous of Lato'na, sent the serpent Python to destroy her. One of the first exploits of Apollo was to kill the Python with his arrows.

Ques. How is this god generally represented?

Ans. As a young man, comely and graceful. He wears a laurel crown over his flowing hair; his garments are embroidered with gold; in his right hand he carries his bow, and bears on his shoulder a quiver filled with arrows. Apollo and his sister Diana presided respectively over the sun and moon. The sun is often called Phœbus, or Apollo, and in ancient pictures the head of the god is represented as darting rays. Apollo, like other divinities, had many names.

Ques. What was the cause of Apollo's being driven from heaven?

Ans. He had a son named Æsculapius, who was so skilled in medicine that he was even able to restore the dead to life. Hippol'ytus, son of Theseus, king of Athens, was killed by sea-monsters. Æsculapius, by bringing him to life, so offended Jupiter that the latter killed him with a thunderbolt. Apollo was much grieved, and, as he could not take revenge on Jupiter, he killed the Cyclops who forged the thunderbolts. For this reason Jupiter banished Apollo from heaven.

Ques. How did he occupy himself in his banishment?

Ans. He guarded the flocks of Admetus, king of Thessaly. Here he had the misfortune accidentally to kill Hyacinthus, a boy to whom he was much attached. Apollo mourned deeply for the youth, and caused a flower to spring from his blood, which is called the hyacinth. Cyparis'sus was also beloved by the god. The boy grieved so deeply at having unintentionally killed a favorite deer, that he begged Apollo to make his mourning perpetual. The god heard his prayer and changed him to a cypress, the branches of which tree were always used at funerals. After many adventures and wanderings, Apollo was restored to the favor of Jupiter, and to heaven.

Ques. What favor did Apollo confer on King Admetus?

Ans. He obtained from the Fates, that when Admetus should be about to end his existence, his life might be prolonged, provided another died willingly in his stead. When the fatal day came, Alcestis, the wife of Admetus, devoted herself to death for her husband. Admetus grieved so deeply at her loss that Proser'pine actually relented, but Pluto remained inexorable. Hercules, however, descended to the shades, and rescued Alcestis, who was restored to her husband. Euripides has founded one of his most beautiful tragedies upon this story.

Ques. Over what sciences did Apollo preside?

Ans. He presided over physic, music, poetry, and rhetoric; and the nine Muses were subject to him. He regulated the day by guiding the chariot of the sun.

Ques. What else is said of Apollo?

Ans. Many absurd and impossible adventures are told. He seems to have been very vain of his musical skill, as we see from the punishment he inflicted on Mar'syas, and King Midas for coming in conflict with him on that point.

Ques. Relate these stories.

Ans. Apollo was challenged by Mar'syas to a contest in music. The god was not content with defeating the presumptious musician, but flayed him alive, and afterwards changed him into a river, which is still known by his name.

The punishment inflicted on King Midas was not so cruel. This prince had the bad taste to declare his preference for the vulgar music of Pan, in a contest which that god had with Apollo. The insulted deity caused his ears to grow in length and shape like those of an ass. Midas endeavored to cover the deformity by his hair, and since it was impossible to conceal it from his barber, he bound him to silence by great promises. This man, however, found it so painful to keep the secret to himself, that to obtain relief, he dug a little hole in the ground, and whispered it to the earth. What was his dismay at hearing the hollow reeds which grew upon the spot, whispering, whenever the wind blew: "King Midas has asses' ears!"

Ques. Is anything else related of King Midas?

Ans. Yes; he had kindly and hospitably entertained Silenus, the preceptor of Bacchus, and in return, the god bade him choose any recompense he pleased. Midas demanded that whatever he should touch might be turned into gold. This prayer was granted, and he was at first overjoyed to see plants, stones and all around him transformed into glittering metal. He soon perceived his folly, however, for when, pressed by hunger, he tried to partake of the food placed before him, it was suddenly converted into gold. and when he would have quenched his thirst, the water was changed into a golden stream. Famished in the midst of plenty, Midas prayed the god to withdraw the fatal gift. Bacchus kindly consented, and ordered him to bathe in the river Pac'tolus. Midas obeyed, but the virtue which left his body was communicated to the waters of the stream, which was famous ever after for its golden sands.

APOLLO.

Ques. Who was Phæton?

Ans. He was the son of Phœbus and Clym'ene. At the earnest solicitation of his mother, he repaired to the palace of the Sun for the purpose of having his parentage publicly acknowledged. The youth was kindly received, and Apollo swore by the Styx to grant him any favor he should ask. Phæton immediately prayed that he might be allowed to drive, for one day only, the chariot of the Sun. Apollo tried to dissuade him from his foolish wish, but in vain. The rash youth was not able to control the fiery horses of the Sun; they departed from their usual track, and heaven and earth were threatened with one universal conflagration. Jupiter perceived the danger, and struck Phæton with a thunderbolt. His body was hurled into the river Po, where it was found and buried by the nymphs of the place. As his sisters were weeping around his tomb, they were changed by Jupiter into poplars.

Ques. Who was Daphne?

Ans. A nymph beloved by Apollo: she was changed into a laurel while she was flying from the pursuit of the god.

Ques. What things were especially sacred to Apollo?

Ans. Among plants, the laurel; among animals, the wolf; and among birds, the hawk, the crow, and the swan were sacred to this god.

CHAPTER IV.

MARS — ARES.

Ques. Who was Mars?

Ans. He was the son of Jupiter and Juno, and was worshipped as the god of war.

Ques. How was he represented?

Ans. As a warrior in splendid armor, standing in a chariot driven by Bello'na, a distracted woman, who holds a torch in her hand. Mars is fierce in aspect and brandishes a spear. Sometimes Discord is represented going before him in tattered garments, while Anger and Clamor follow in his train. Fear and Terror are the horses which draw the chariot.

Ques. What animals were sacred to Mars?

Ans. The dog, on account of its sagacity in the pursuit of prey; the horse, for its uses in war; the wolf, for its rapacity and cruelty; the raven, because it follows armies, watching for the carcasses of the slain; and the cock, as an emblem of the vigilance which guards against surprise.

Ques. What other names had Mars?

Ans. He was called Quiri'nus when he was quiet, Gradi'vus when he was raging; therefore the Romans built him two temples, one to Mars Quiri'nus within the walls, that he might keep the city in peace; and one without, to Mars Gradi'vus, that he might defend them against their enemies. Among the Romans, priests called Salii attended to the sacrifices of Mars, and on festival days went about the city dancing with their shields. Their name comes from the Latin word "to dance," and was considered appropriate, because Mars is inconstant in his temper, and inclines now to this side, now to that, in time of war. Except the story of his attachment to Venus, the poets relate but little of Mars.

Bellona, the goddess of war, was, according to some, the sister of Mars. She is generally represented as above, but some poets have described her as rushing through the ranks of war, waving a flaming torch, and exciting the combatants by her cries. The temple of Bellona at Rome, was without the city, near the Carmental gate. Here the Senate gave audience to such ambassadors as they were not willing to admit within the walls. A pillar stood before the temple, over which the herald cast a spear when he proclaimed war. The priests of Bellona, when officiating, held naked swords, with which they gashed their arms and shoulders, making libations of their own blood, to the terrible goddess.

CHAPTER V.

MERCURY—HERMES.

Ques. Who was Mercury?

Ans. He was the son of Jupiter and Ma'ia, the daughter of Atlas. On his mother's account, sacrifices were generally offered to him during the month of May.

Ques. How is Mercury represented?

Ans. As a young man of cheerful countenance, having wings fixed to his helmet and his sandals, and carrying a rod in his hand, which is also winged, and entwined with serpents.

Ques. How are these different equipments named?

Ans. The rod was called Cadu'ceus, and possessed a wonderful faculty for quieting all disputes. His helmet was called Pet'asus, and his winged sandals Talaria.

Ques. What were the offices of Mercury?

Ans. They were various; his most important function was to carry the commands of Jupiter. Mercury is commonly called the messenger of the gods. He also swept the room where the gods supped, and made their beds.

MERCURY. 37

Ques. What else is said of Mercury?

Ans. He was the inventor of letters, and excelled in eloquence. The Greeks worshipped him as the patron of orators, under the name of Hermes. Mercury was also the inventor of weights and measures, and the patron of commerce.

Ques. Were all his talents equally honorable.

Ans. No; he was most skillful in the art of thieving. On the very day of his birth, he stole some cattle from King Admetus, although Apollo was keeping them; and while that god was bending his bow against him, he contrived to steal his quiver. While yet an infant, he stole the tools of Vulcan, the girdle of Venus, and the sceptre of Jupiter. He intended also to steal Jove's thunderbolts, but was fearful they would burn him. Mercury was, therefore, the patron of thieves.

Ques. Relate the history of Io and Argus?

Ans. Io, the daughter of In'achus, was beloved by Jupiter. He strove to hide her from the anger of Juno by transforming her into a cow. The goddess suspected the deceit, and begged the beautiful heifer as a gift. Jupiter was afraid to refuse, and Juno consigned the unhappy Io to the guardianship of Argus. Escape seemed hopeless, as Argus had a hundred eyes, of which he closed only two in sleep, while the others watched. Jupiter commanded Mercury to slay Argus and deliver Io. To effect this, it was necessary to set all his eyes to sleep. Mercury disguised himself as a shepherd, entered into conversation with Argus, and at length played so sweetly on his pipe, that, one by one, the keeper's hundred eyes were closed. The god then drew his falchion, and cut off the head of Argus with a single blow. Juno was grieved for her servant, and placed his eyes in her peacock's tail. Io, still persecuted by Juno, wandered over the earth, and at length arrived, faint and weary, on the banks of the Nile. There she prayed Jupiter either to restore her to her original form, or to terminate her misfortunes by death. Juno was touched with compassion, and allowed Jupiter to grant her request. Io was restored to human form, and married to Osiris, king of Egypt; she was afterwards worshipped in that country under the name of **Isis**.

The statues of Mercury were simply wooden posts, surmounted by a rude head with a pointed beard. They were set up in the fields, and at all cross roads. The Greeks had pillars of stone, which they called Hermæ, but the head which surmounted them was not always that of Mercury. These pillars were sometimes placed, by the Athenians, at the entrances of their houses as a protection against thieves. On one occasion, all the Hermæ in Athens were mutilated in the same night. Alcibiades was accused of this sacrilege, and was obliged to take refuge in Cergos, from the indignation of the people.

CHAPTER VI.

BACCHUS—DIONYSUS.

Ques. Who was Bacchus?

Ans. He was the son of Jupiter and Sem'ele and was worshipped as the god of wine.

Ques. How is he represented?

Ans. As a young man, crowned with ivy and grape leaves; he sits in a chariot, drawn sometimes by panthers and lynxes, and sometimes by tigers and lions. He carries in his hand a thyrsus—that is, a staff encircled by ivy and grape leaves; a troop of demons and drunken satyrs follow him.

Ques. What was the story of Sem'ele?

Ans. She was destroyed by the jealousy of Juno. This goddess visited Sem'ele in the shape of an old woman, and persuaded her to ask Jupiter to visit her with all the glory which encompassed him in heaven. All happened as Juno desired, and Sem'ele was consumed by the lightnings which surrounded Jupiter. Bacchus did not share his mother's fate, but was conveyed to Naxos, where he was educated by some nymphs

Ques. How did Bacchus reward their care?

Ans. He transformed them into the stars known as the Hyades.

Ques. Who aided the nymphs in their care of Bacchus?

Ans. An old man named Silenus. He was considered a demi-god.

Ques. How is Silenus represented?

Ans. He seems to be the personfication of drunkenness; he is sometimes represented as seated intoxicated on a cask of wine, his head crowned with grape leaves, and his face stained with the lees of wine; sometimes as mounted on an ass, and following the car of Bacchus.

Ques. What were the first exploits of Bacchus?

Ans. He distinguished himself in the combats between the gods and giants, taking the form of a lion to strike terror into the latter.

Ques. What other actions are attributed to him?

Ans. He taught men how to plant the vine and till the ground. He is said to have subdued India, and many other countries of the East.

Ques. How was he worshipped?

Ans. The goat and the hog were offered to him in sacrifice; and the ivy, the fir, the bindweed, the fig and the vine were consecrated to him.

Ques. What feasts where held in his honor?

Ans. The feasts of Bacchus were various. The Bacchanalia or Orgia were the most celebrated. They were at first participated in by women only out afterwards men were admitted to join in these rites. The women were called Bacchantes, and ran about with their hair dishevelled, shouting and singing in a distracted manner. The Roman Senate at length abolished this festival.

Ques. Relate the story of Pentheus?

Ans. Pentheus was king of Thebes. He not only refused to acknowledge the divinity of Bacchus, but endeavored to prevent the celebration of his orgies. Having presumed to intrude on the revels of the Bacchantes, they were seized by a sort of madness, and rushing upon the unhappy man, tore him to pieces. The mother of Pentheus, and her sisters, were the leaders in this act, which was considered to have been performed under a divine impulse.

Ques. What was the punishment inflicted on Alcitho'e and her sisters?

Ans. These were Theban maidens who ridiculed the orgies of Bacchus. During the celebration of these rites, they remained at home, plying the distaff and the spindle, and singing over their tasks. For this, Alcitho'e and her sisters were transformed by the power of Bacchus into bats; and the spindle and yarn with which they worked were changed to ivy.

Ques. Relate the transformation of mariners into dolphins?

Ans. A ship touched at Chios for a supply of fresh water. The sailors who went on shore, found near the spring a boy of uncommon grace and beauty. They bore him to the ship, still heavy with sleep and wine, and declared their intention of selling him at the next port. Acœ'tes, their captain, tried to dissuade them from the crime, the more so, as he perceived that there was something more than mortal about the captive youth. In the meantime Bacchus, for it was he, awaking from his slumber, begged the sailors to land him at Naxos. This the captain promised, but when they had set sail, the mariners took possession of the ship, and steered in another direction. The god now revealed himself. The sails and cordage suddenly appeared hung with grapes and ivy; spotted panthers lay at his feet, and when the terrified sailors tried to leap overboard, they were suddenly changed into dolphins. The captain was spared, and landed with Bacchus on the shores of Chios.

Ques. What is the origin of the history of Bacchus?

Ans. He was probably some prince who taught the people to till the ground, and cultivate the vine. They disgraced his memory in after times by the drunken revels they held in his honor.

CHAPTER VII.

Celestial Goddesses.

JUNO—HERA.

Ques. Who was Juno?

Ans. She was the daughter of Saturn and Ops, and was both sister and wife of Jupiter.

Ques. How is she generally represented?

Ans. As seated in a golden chariot drawn by peacocks. She holds a sceptre in her hand, and is crowned with roses and lilies. Iris was the messenger of Juno, as Mercury was of Jupiter.

Ques. How is Iris represented?

Ans. With wings, because of her swiftness, and sometimes also as riding on a rainbow.

Ques. How did Iris differ from Mercury?

Ans. Mercury was often employed in messages of peace; but Iris was frequently sent to promote strife and dissension.

Ques. What children had Juno?

Ans. Vulcan, Mars and Hebe. Hebe was called the goddess of youth, on account of her extraordinary beauty, and Jupiter made her his cup-bearer. She offended him by an unlucky fall, and Ganymede was appointed in her place.

Ques. What were Juno's faults?

Ans. She was very jealous, and took the most cruel revenge on the mortal woman whom Jupiter loved. She transformed Callista and her son Arcas into bears, and was extremely displeased when Jupiter placed them among the constellations.

The goddess carried her complaint to Ocean'us, bidding him to observe, when the shades of night should darken the world, how her rival was exalted. The god of Ocean was moved, and promised Juno that he would never receive either Callista or her offspring in his watery domain. Hence it is, that the Greater and the Lesser Bear continually circle around the pole, and never sink, like the other stars, beneath the waves of ocean. In the fables of Bacchus and Hercules, Juno displays the same character, extending to these heroes the enmity she bore their mortal mothers.

Juno was chiefly honored at Argos, Samos and Platæa. The victims offered to her were kine, ewe lambs, and sows. The cow was consecrated to her, and at Argos the priestess of Juno always rode in a chariot drawn by oxen. The sacred plants of the goddess were, the willow, pome granate, the dittany and the lily. The peacock was chosen as the bird of Juno, because it was supposed by its cry to indicate a change of weather.

CHAPTER VIII.

MINERVA—PALLAS ATHENA.

Ques. Who was Minerva?

Ans. She was the goddess of wisdom and of war. She had no mother, but sprang full armed from the head of Jupiter.

Ques. How is Minerva represented?

Ans. As clothed in complete armor. She has a golden helmet on her head, holds a lance in her right hand, and her left rests upon a shield to which is affixed the head of Medusa. The cock and the owl are also represented on the shield.

Ques. Why was Minerva said to have sprung full armed from the head of Jupiter?

Ans. The poets signify by this, that wisdom comes direct from the deity.

Ques. Why is Minerva sometimes crowned with olive?

Ans. Because the olive is the emblem of peace, and war should only be made that a secure peace may follow; also because she bestowed the olive on men.

Ques. On what occasion did Minerva give the olive to men?

Ans. When Cecrops built a new city, Neptune and Minerva contended about its name; and it was resolved that whichever of the two deities should confer the most useful gift on man, might give a name to the city. Neptune struck the ground with his trident, and a horse appeared; but Minerva caused an olive to spring out of the earth. The latter was judged the more useful gift; and Minerva named the city, calling it Athe′na or Athens, after her own name in Greek.

Ques. What was the Palladium?

Ans. When the Trojans were building the temple and castle of Minerva in Troy, a statue of the goddess fell from heaven into the castle, which was still unroofed. The oracle of Apollo declared that Troy would be safe so long as this statue, called Palladium, from Pallas, a name of Minerva, remained within the walls. When the Greeks besieged Troy, they found that all their efforts to take the city were of no avail; they determed, therefore, to steal the Palladium. Ulysses and Diom′edes crept into the city through the common sewers, and brought away the image. Troy was soon afterwards taken and destroyed. Minerva was a virgin, and was the patroness of modest and virtuous women.

Ques. Did Minerva excel only in the art of war?

Ans. No; she invented the distaff and spindle,

and excelled in every branch of female industry. The fate of Arach'ne shows how much she prized her reputation for skill in embroidery.

Ques. Who was Arach'ne?

Ans. She was a maiden of Lydia, who had the presumption to challenge Minerva to a trial of skill in weaving. The goddess wrought into her work the most beautiful designs, but it would seem that Arach'ne's performance surpassed hers: for Minerva, seeing it, was fired with envy, and struck the unhappy maiden on the face with her shuttle. Arach'ne could not endure this insult, and hung herself from a beam. Minerva immediately changed her into a spider, and permitted her to live only that she might weave unceasingly.

Ques. Why was the owl chosen as the bird of Minerva?

Ans. because this bird sees in the dark; and wisdom distinguishes what is hidden from common eyes.

Ques. What is the story of Medu'sa's head?

Ans. Medusa was one of three sisters, the daughters of Phorcus. These maidens were called Gorgons, and were all immortal, except Medu'sa. The latter was at one period distinguished for her personal beauty, and particularly for her flowing hair; but having offended Minerva, that goddess changed her locks into serpents, and rendered her appearance so frightful that all who beheld her were changed to stone. The hero Perseus undertook an expedition against the Gorgons, and as he saw the whole country around covered with figures of men and animals changed into stone by the sight of the monster, he was obliged to use great precaution to avoid the same misfortune. He looked, therefore, not at Medu'sa, but at her reflection in his polished shield, and when he perceived that she was asleep, Minerva guiding his sword, he struck off her head. Mercury had lent Perseus his wings, and as he flew over the Lybian desert bearing Medu'sa's head, the blood fell upon the burning sands, and produced the serpents which have ever since infested that region. From the blood of Medu'sa, also, when her head was cut off, sprang the famous winged horse called Peg'asus. This wonderful steed flew to Mount Helicon, the residence of the Muses, where, by striking the earth with his foot, he produced the fountain Hippocre'ne. All who drank of its waters were inspired by the Muses with a poetic spirit. Perseus went through many other adventures in which Medu'sa's head did him good service, by changing his enemies into stone. He afterwards gave the head to Minerva, who fixed it on her shield.

CHAPTER IX.

VENUS—APHRODITE.

Ques. Who was Venus?

Ans. She was the goddess of love and beauty She sprang from the froth of the sea; for this reason the Greeks called her Aphrodi'te, from Aphros, meaning foam. As soon as she was born, she was placed like a pearl in a shell instead of a cradle, and the god Zephyrus (the west wind) wafted her to the shores of Cyprus.

Ques. By whom was she educated?

Ans. She was educated and adorned by the Horæ or Hours, who carried her to heaven as soon she became of age. All the gods were astonished at the beauty of Venus, and many demanded her in marriage; but Jupiter betrothed her to Vulcan, an ugly and deformed divinity.

Ques. How is Venus represented?

Ans. Sometimes as a young virgin rising from the sea, or riding on the waves in a shell, while Cupids, Nereids and Dolphins are sporting around her—again, she is pictured as traversing the heavens in an ivory chariot drawn by doves.

She wears a wonderful girdle called the Cestus her doves are harnessed with golden chains, and Cupids flutter around her on silken wings. Venus is always crowned with roses.

Ques. What was there remarkable in the Cestus of Venus?

Ans. It had the property of conferring grace, beauty, and irresistible attractions on the wearer.

Ques. Where had Venus temples?

Ans. In many places. The most celebrated were at Paphos, Cytherea, Idalia and Cnidos.

Ques. Who were the companions of Venus?

Ans. The Graces were her attendants, and she was generally accompanied by her son Cupid, who was the god of love.

Ques. How is Cupid represented?

Ans. As a beautiful boy with wings, carrying a bow and arrows; he has sometimes a band over his eyes to show that love is blind.

Ques. What do you say of the festivals of Venus?.

Ans. They were various, and accompanied by much that was disgraceful and immoral. The swan, the dove, and the sparrow were sacred to this goddess; and among plants, the rose, the myrtle and the apple. Incense, fruits and flowers were the ordinary sacrifices laid on her altars but birds were sometimes offered.

Ques. What remarkable temple was raised to Venus in Rome?

Ans. There was a temple dedicated to Venus

Calva, or the Bald; because when the Gauls besieged Rome, the inhabitants made ropes for their military engines with the long hair of the Roman women.

Ques. On what occasion was the prize of beauty adjudged to Venus?

Ans. All the gods and goddesses had been invited to the marriage of Peleus and Thetis, Discordia, or Discord being the only one excluded. This goddess was determined to revenge the slight; she entered secretly, when all were assembled, and threw among them a golden apple on which was written: "For the fairest." A violent quarrel immediately arose between the goddesses, for each believed herself to be the most beautiful. Juno, Minerva, and Venus disputed so eagerly, that Jupiter himself was not able to bring them to an agreement. He resolved, therefore, to refer the matter to the decision of Paris, who was then feeding his sheep on Mount Ida. This prince was the son of Priam, king of Troy. An oracle had foretold before his birth that he was destined to cause the destruction of his native city. He was, therefore, exposed on Mount Ida, where he was found and cared for by some shepherds. After he had grown up, he acquired a great reputation for the prudence with which he settled the most difficult disputes; hence the difference between the goddesses was referred to his decision. When they appeared before him, they began to court his favor with promises. Juno offered him great power; Minerva, wisdom; but Venus promised to give him for a wife the most beautiful woman in the world. Paris then pronounced Venus the fairest. He was soon after acknowledged by his father, King Priam; and Venus fulfilled her engagement by aiding him to carry off Helen, the beautiful wife of Menela'us, king of Sparta. This gave rise to the total destruction of Troy; and the prediction of the oracle with regard to Paris was accomplished.

Ques. What was the story of Hippo'menes and Atalanta?

Ans. Atalanta was the daughter of King Cœneus, and was equally renowned for her beauty and her swiftness in running. As an oracle had declared that marriage would be fatal to her, she freed herself from the importunity of her suitors by a singular expedient. She caused it to be proclaimed that any one who sought her hand should contend with her in running, with the understanding that she would marry him who should excel her in the race, but that those who were beaten should suffer death. Hard as were these conditions, many suitors presented themselves, but they were all unsuccessful, and were put to death without mercy. Hippo'menes determined to undertake the race, but first, he had recourse to Venus. This goddess gave him three golden apples gathered in the garden of the Hesper'ides, and directed him as to their use. When Hippomenes saw that Atalanta was going to outstrip him in the race, he threw down a golden apple; the princess paused to admire and take up the glittering fruit, while Hippo'menes passed on. A second and a third time did he try the same expedient, and with such success that he reached the goal and won his bride. Hippo'menes was ungrateful to Venus, who revenged herself by changing him into a lion, and the beautiful Atalanta into a lioness.

Ques. Who was Adonis?

Ans. He was a beautiful youth, the son of Cin'yras, king of Cyprus, and was beloved by Venus. He was killed by a wild boar, while hunting with that goddess. Venus grieved much for her favorite. To commemorate his cruel fate she caused the flower anemone to spring from his blood.

According to the poets, the rose was formerly white. When Venus was hastening to the assistance of Adonis, her foot was wounded by a thorn, and some drops of blood fell upon that flower, which then assumed its present crimson hue.

Ques. Who were the Graces?

Ans. They were inferior goddesses, who presided over the banquet, the dance and all social enjoyments and elegant arts.

Ques. How many were there?

Ans. They were three in number. Their names were Euphro'syne, Agla'ia and Thalia. They are represented as beautiful young women, standing in graceful attitudes with their hands joined.

CHAPTER X.

LATONA—LETO.

Ques. Who was Latona?

Ans. She was the daughter of Phœbe and Cœus the Titan. When she was driven from heaven by the jealousy of Juno, she found an asylum in the island of Delos, where she gave birth to Apollo and Diana. Terra (the earth) had promised Juno to give no shelter to her rival, but the island of Delos formerly floated in the sea, and was at that time hidden under the waters. Neptune, pitying the forlorn state of Latona, caused it to emerge from the sea, when it became fixed and immovable for her use.

Ques. Relate the transformation of Lycian peasants into frogs.

Ans. Latona, while wandering with her babes in the country of Lycia, in Asia, arrived, exhausted by heat and fatigue, on the borders of a clear pool. She was about to quench her thirst in the cool waters, when some clowns rudely hindered her. She begged them to have compassion, and not deny her so small a refreshment;

but they mocked her prayers, and when she tried to approach they waded into the pool, and, stiring up the mud, defiled the waters so that it became unfit to drink. The goddess was so much incensed, that she changed the cruel rustics into frogs, and condemned them to dwell forever in the muddy pool.

The punishment of Niobe will be related in another place. The sufferings of the giant Tityus in hell, were also the penalty of an insult offered to this goddess.

The Greeks personified Night, under the name of Latona; hence she was said to have been the first wife of Jupiter, the mother of Apollo and Diana, (the sun and moon) and the nurse of the earth and stars. The Egyptians had the same allegory, with a little variation, as, according to them, she was grandmother and nurse of Horus and Bu'bastis, their Apollo and Diana.

This goddess is generally represented on ancient monuments, as a large and beautiful woman, wearing a veil. In paintings, the veil is always black; in cutting gems, artists sometimes availed themselves of a dark colored vein in the stone, to produce the same effect, and represent the shades of night. The veil is sometimes studded with stars.

CHAPTER XL.

AURORA—EOS.

Ques. Who was Aurora?

Ans. She was the goddess of the morning and sister of the sun and moon. She is represented as seated in a golden chariot drawn by milk-white horses; her countenance is brilliant, and her fingers are red like roses.

Ques. What did this represent?

Ans. The beauty of the morning heavens.

Ques. Relate the story of Ceph'alus and Procris.

Ans. Ceph'alus, a beautiful youth, was beloved by Aurora, who carried him with her to heaven; but he regarded the goddess with indifference, and insisted on returning to his young wife Procris. Aurora allowed him to depart, but prevailed on him to visit his house in disguise, that he might judge of the constancy of his bride. Ceph'alus found his wife lamenting his absence and refusing all consolation, but when she discovered her husband in the supposed stranger, she was so indignant at his suspicion that she fled from him and joined the attendants of Diana. She was afterwards reconciled to Ceph'alus, and gave him two presents which she had received from Diana. These were, a dog that was always sure of its prey, and an arrow which never missed its aim, and returned immediately to the hand of the owner. Ceph'alus was extremely fond of hunting, and when fatigued, he often rested in the shade and invited the presence of "Aura," or the refreshing breeze. This word was mistaken for the name of a nymph by some persons who carried the tale to Procris. Being jealous in her turn, she determined to watch, and discover her rival. When Ceph'alus returned from hunting, Procris concealed herself in the grove; she started upon hearing the name Aura, and caused a rustling among the leaves. Ceph'alus immediately threw his unerring dart, which returned to his hand stained with the blood of his beloved wife. He hastened to the spot, but it was too late, and Procris expired in his arms, acknowledging she had fallen a victim to her own groundless jealousy.

Ques. To whom was Aurora married?

Ans. She chose for her husband Titho'nus, the son of Laom'edon, king of Troy. This prince was endowed with wonderful beauty; but when Aurora begged of Jove that he might be exempted from death, she forgot to ask at the same time for the bloom of immortal youth. When Titho'nus became old and decrepit, Aurora still watched over him with the tenderest care, " giving him ambrosial food and fair garments." When Titho'nus could no longer move his aged limbs, and his feeble voice was scarcely heard, the goddess was moved with compassion, and changed him into a grasshopper.

Ques. Who was Memnon?

Ans. He was king of the Ethiopians, and son of Titho'nus and Aurora. When Troy was besieged, Memnon came with an army to aid the kindred of his father. In the first engagements he slew Antil'ochus, the son of Nestor, and threw the whole army of the Greeks into disorder. Ach'illes, however, appeared on the field, and changed the fortune of the day. The Trojans were routed in their turn, and Memnon fell by the hand of the Grecian hero. Aurora watched the combat from the heavens, and when she saw Memnon fall she directed the winds to convey his body to the banks of the river Æse'pus in Paphlagonia. Here they raised his tomb in a sacred grove, and his obsequies were celebrated with solemn pomp. The sparks, as they rose from the funeral pyre, were changed into birds, which divided into two flocks, and fought together until they fell into the flames and were consumed. According to the poets, Aurora was never consoled for the loss of her son; she mourns unceasingly, and the drops which sparkle in the morning on the grass and flowers are the tears which the goddess continues to shed during the long hours of night. Ancient history mentions many persons of the name of Memnon, particularly a general who distinguished himself in Persia against Alexander the Great. The Memnon of fable was in all probability an Egyptian, and not an Ethiopian king. His statue is still an object of curiosity to travellers.

Ques. Where is this statue, and for what is it remarkable?

Ans. It is one of two colossal figures which are directly opposite the great temple of Luxor. They are called by the Arabs, Shama and Dama. The statue of Memnon is the more northerly of the two, and was formerly celebrated for its vocal powers.

It is commonly asserted by ancient writers that when the first rays of the rising sun fell upon this statue, it acknowledged the presence of Aurora, and uttered a sound like the sudden breaking of a harp-string. By some, it was compared to a blow struck on hollow brass.

Ques. Was there any foundation for such a belief?

Ans. It appeared quite certain that the sounds of which we have spoken, were really heard from this statue at sunrise; the only question is as to the means by which they were produced. The Colossus, although in a sitting posture, measures fifty-two feet in height, and the throne on which it rests is thirty feet long and eighteen broad. These dimensions were sufficient to admit of any internal machinery that might be required to produce the mysterious sounds. Such was the supposition of the Persian king Cambyses, who had the statue cleft asunder from the head to the middle of the body, but without discovering anything. Humboldt conjectured that the sound might be attributed to the nature of the stone, or to the action of the sun's rays upon the air confined in the cavities of the statue. A much more reasonable solution of the mystery has been furnished by Mr. Wilkinson, an intelligent English traveller. He discovered in the lap of the statue a stone, which, on being struck, emits a metallic sound. There is a hollow space hewn in the block behind this stone, sufficiently large to admit of a person lying within it, entirely concealed from observation. Mr. Wilkinson tried the experiment, and was convinced that he had discovered the secret of this famous statue.

The face of the Memnon, like that of the Sphinx has been mutilated by the Arabs; the positions of the figures which are yet uninjured show that the whole must have presented a beautiful and imposing appearance. The base of the throne is covered with ancient inscriptions in Greek and Latin, commemorating the visits of different illustrious persons, and testifying that they had heard the mysterious voice of Memnon.

CHAPTER XII.

Terrestrial Gods.

SATURN.

Ques. Who was Saturn?

Ans. He was the son of Cœlum and **Terra**. He was married to Ops, or Rhea, and was the father of Jupiter, Neptune and Pluto. As we have already learned, Saturn devoured the rest of his male children.

Ques. How is he represented?

Ans. Saturn is represented as an old man armed with a scythe, which signifies that time mows down everything in its course; and he holds in his hands an infant which he is about to devour, because time destroys all that it brings forth.

Ques. How did Saturn lose his kingdom?

Ans. He was deposed by Jupiter, and was obliged to take refuge in Italy, where he taught the people the arts of civilized life. Janus, king of Italy, made Saturn partner of his kingdom, and that part of the country was called Latium, from a Latin word which meant to hide; it was sometimes also called Saturnia. Saturn's government was so wise and beneficial that his reign was called the Golden Age. The poets tell us that all men then lived on a perfect equality, property was held in common, and the earth brought forth its fruits without labor.

Ques. What sacrifices were offered to Saturn?

Ans. He was worshipped with human sacrifices, which seems strange when we consider that he was so mild a king. The planet Saturn was supposed by the ancients to exercise a malignant influence.

Ques. What were the Saturnalia?

Ans. They were solemnities instituted by Tullus Hostilius, king of Rome. In early times the festival lasted one day, but after Julius Cæsar, it was prolonged to three, four, or five days.

Ques. How were these days observed?

Ans. They were a season of general rejoicing; the Senate did not sit, schools gave holidays, and friends sent presents to one another. It was unlawful to proclaim war or execute criminals during this festival. Servants might, at this time, say what they pleased to their masters, who could not take offence; also, in memory of the freedom and equality enjoyed in Saturn's reign, they sat at table while their masters served, and reproved the latter freely if they were guilty of any awkwardness. Lastly, servants and common people were allowed to wear purple cloaks, a distinction reserved at other times to the patricians. The

SATURN.

Saturnalia is probably represented in some degree by the modern Carnival. Saturn is thought by some persons to have been the same as Noah.

JANUS.

Ques. Who was Janus?

Ans. He was an ancient Italian deity, of whose origin very contradictory accounts are given. He was supposed to have reigned in Italy in the time of Saturn, and to have associated that god with him in the kingdom. He was generally represented with two faces, and was called hence, Janus Bifrons. He had many temples in Rome. The gates of the chief temple, that of Janus Quiri'nus, were always open in time of war, and closed when the Romans were at peace. It is a remarkable circumstance that the gates of Janus were closed but three times in seven hundred years. They were shut for the first time in the reign of Numa; again, after the first Punic war; and Augustus closed the temple the third time when he had given peace to the world. This occurred just before the coming of our Lord. The first month of the year is named from Janus

CHAPTER XIII.

VULCAN—HAPHÆSTUS.

Ques. Who was Vulcan?

Ans. He was the son of Jupiter and Juno, but was cast down from heaven on account of his deformed appearance. He landed in Lemnos, but broke his leg in the fall, and remained lame ever afterwards.

Ques. How was Vulcan represented?

Ans. As a smith standing by an anvil with tools in his hand.

Ques. What was his occupation?

Ans. He had a blacksmith shop in Lemnos, were he manufactured Jupiter's thunderbolts, and the arms of the other gods. Vulcan was the god of fire, and the patron of blacksmiths and armorers.

Ques. What were the most celebrated works of Vulcan?

Ans. The armor of Ach'illes and of Æ'neas, the beautiful necklace of Hermi'one, the crown of Ariadne, and the brazen palace of the sun. The shield of Ach'illes was enamelled with metals of various colors, and embossed with beautiful historical designs.

Ques. To whom was Vulcan married?

Ans. Vulcan was married to Venus, but that goddess behaved treacherously towards him and attached herself to Mars.

Ques. Who were the servants of Vulcan?

Ans. The attendants of Vulcan were called Cyclops, because they had each one eye in the middle of the forehead; they were the offspring of Neptune and Amphitri'te.

Ques. How was Vulcan worshipped?

Ans. The Romans celebrated feasts in his honor called Vulcania. At these they sacrificed animals by throwing them into the fire to be burned to death. The Athenians also kept feasts of Vulcan, and there was in Sicily, upon Mount Etna, a famous temple dedicated to him.

Ques. What was peculiar about this temple?

Ans. The approach to it was guarded by dogs, whose scent was so keen that they could discover whether the persons coming to the temple were virtuous or wicked. To the servants of Vulcan might be added Cacus, who stole the oxen of Hercules; and the robber Cæ'culus, from whom the noble Roman family of the Cæcilii derived their name. He was the founder of the city of Præneste One fable is, that certain shepherds found Cæ'culus, when an infant, lying unhurt in a glowing fire, from which circumstance he was supposed to be the son of Vulcan. The shepherd, Polyphemus, resembled the Cyclops, and was, like them, a son of Neptune. The monster devoured several of the companions of Ulysses, but the hero, having made him drunk with wine, put out his single eye with a firebrand and escaped. He embarked in haste, pursued by the monster; his companions shouted defiance as they weighed anchor, and the blind Cyclops, directed by the sound of their voices, hurled a rock into the sea, by which their vessel was almost swamped. Warned by this danger, they rowed silently until they reached the open sea. Some writers have imagined that the Cyclops were a race of miners, who, descending into the deep recesses of the earth, and coming forth again, had a lamp attached to their foreheads, to give them light. This, at a distance, would appear like a large, flaming eye, and might give rise to the fable of one-eyed monsters. This explanation is, however, far fetched and improbable.

Ques. Can you name any works of Vulcan, beside those already mentioned?

Ans. Yes, he made for Alcinoûs, king of the Phæacians, gold and silver dogs which guarded his house. To Minos, king of Crete, he gave th brazen man Talus, who passed around the island three times every day, to guard it from invasion. For himself, Vulcan formed golden handmaidens, whom he endowed with reason and speech.

CHAPTER XIV.

ÆOLUS.

Ques. Who was Æ'olus?

Ans. He was the god of the winds; he could imprison them in a dark cave, or, by setting them free, create tempests.

Ques. What was the origin of this fable?

Ans. It is believed that Æ'olus was a skillful astronomer who dwelt in a volcanic island. By noticing the clouds of smoke, and how they rose, he was enabled to foretell storms a long time before they happened; hence the ignorant believed that he could bring high winds and tempests whenever he pleased.

MOMUS.

Ques. Who was Momus?

Ans. He was the son of Night and Sleep; the name Momus signifies a jester. His occupation was to criticise the other gods, and censure their actions.

Ques. Give an example?

Ans. Neptune, Vulcan, and Minerva contended for the prize of skill; Neptune made a bull, Minerva a house, and Vulcan a man. Momus was called upon to decide their merits, but he blamed them all. He said that Neptune was imprudent in not placing the bull's horns in his forehead, before his eyes, that he might give a stronger and surer blow. He found fault with Minerva's house, because it was immovable and could not be carried away if it were placed among bad neighbors. He said that Vulcan was the worst of all, because he did not put a window in the man's breast so that his thoughts might be seen. No god could escape the censure of Momus. When he could find nothing to criticise in the person of Venus, he complained of the noise made by her golden sandals. **Momus was at length driven from Olympus.**

CHAPTER XV.

Terrestrial Goddesses.

VESTA—HESTIA

Ques. Who was Vesta?

Ans. She was the daughter of Saturn and Ops or Rhea, and was, therefore, the sister of Jupiter. She was considered the guardian of homes and firesides, and was a household divinity. Statues of Vesta were placed by the Romans at the entrance of their houses; hence the word vestibule, which we still use.

Ques. How is Vesta usually represented?

Ans. As seated on the ground, and leaning upon a drum, while various domestic animals are grouped about her.

Ques. What was the character of this goddess?

Ans. She was esteemed very holy, and was the patroness of household virtues. When Jupiter asked her to choose whatever gift she would, Vesta desired that she might remain always a virgin, and receive the first oblations in all sacrifices Fire was the emblem of this goddess, and in her temple, at Rome, a sacred fire was suspended in the air, and watched by the Vestal Virgins. If this fire chanced to be extinguished, all public and private business was suspended until the accident had been expiated.

Ques. What laws existed with regard to the Vestal Virgins?

Ans. The penalties for neglect of their duties were severe. If the sacred fire was extinguished through their negligence, they were sometimes cruelly punished, and if any Virgin infringed the rule which forbade her to marry, she was buried alive; being shut up in a vault underground, with a lamp, and a little bread, wine, water and oil. The sacred fire of Vesta was watched by these priestesses for nearly eleven centuries. We are told that during this period, twenty Vestals were condemned to death. Of these, seven were permitted to take their own lives, thirteen suffered the terrible punishment we have described. The last execution of this kind took place in the reign of the emperor Domitian.

Ques. What were the privileges of the Vestal Virgins?

Ans. In recompense for these severe laws, the Vestals were treated with extraordinary respect. They had the most honorable seats at games and festivals, and even the consuls and magistrates gave them precedence; their testimony was taken in trials without any form of oath, and if they happened to meet a criminal going to execution, he was immediately pardoned. Public documents of great importance were generally entrusted to their care.

A striking instance of the respect felt for these Virgins, is related by a Roman historian. Appius Claudius Audax, a consul who had rendered himself obnoxious to the people, was attacked in the midst of a triumphal procession by the plebeian tribunes, who endeavored to pull him from his chariot. His daughter, who was a Vestal Virgin ascended the triumphal car, and took her place by her father's side. The tumult immediately subsided, and the procession proceeded quietly to the capital.

Ques. How many Vestal Virgins were there?

Ans. The number has been variously stated. Some authors mention six, others seven, as the number actually in office. They were chosen between the ages of six and ten; for ten years they were employed in learning their duty; they remained in office for ten, and ten other years were employed in instructing the novices. If there were seven Vestals always in office, the entire number must have been twenty-one. The thirty years being ended, the Vestals returned to their families. The law then permitted them to marry, but it was considered discreditable to do so.

CHAPTER XVI.

CYBELE

Ques. Who was Cyb'ele?

Ans. This goddess, sometimes called by the Greeks, Rhea, and by the Latins, Ops, is considered to be a personification of the earth. She is goddess, not of cities only, but of all things which the earth contains. She was the **daughter of Cœlum**, and the wife of **Saturn**.

Ques. How was Cyb'ele represented?

Ans. Generally as riding in a chariot, drawn by lions. She wears a turreted crown, and is clothed in a many-colored mantle, on which are represented the figures of various animals. In her right hand she holds a sceptre, and in her left, a key. This last emblem seems to signify that the earth locks up her treasures in the winter season. Cyb'ele is always represented with the dignified and matronly air which distinguishes Juno and Ceres.

Ques. How was she worshipped?

Ans. Sacrifices were first offered to this goddess in Phrygia and Lydia. Her temples were gener-

CYBELE. 73

ally built on the summits of mountains; that on Mount Dindymus near Pessi'nus, in Galatia, was particularly celebrated. Her statue in this temple was simply a large aerolite which had fallen in the vicinity, and was regarded by the people as the heaven-sent image of their great goddess. At the close of the second Punic war, the Romans, directed, it is said, by the Sibylline books, sent an embassy to Attalus, king of Pergamus, requesting that he would permit the so-called image to be removed to Rome. The monarch consented, and the sacred stone was carried in triumph to the Italian capital. There it was placed in a stately temple built for the purpose, and a solemn festival, called Megalesia, was celebrated annually, in honor of Cyb'ele. During these solemnities, priests called Galli and Corybantes ran about like madmen, with cries and howlings, making, at the same time, a terrific noise with the clashing of cymbals, the sound of pipes and other instruments. In their frenzy, they cut their flesh with knives, and performed many other extravagances, but the people regarded them with reverence, as they were believed, while in this state, to possess the gift of prophecy.

The divinity worshipped by the Roman women under the name of Bona Dea, or Good Goddess, is believed to be the same as Cyb'ele.

Ancient writers relate an extraordinary incident connected with the arrival of the image of Cyb'ele in Rome. The ship which bore the sacred stone was stranded on a shoal in the Tiber. Claudia, a Vestal Virgin who was suspected of having violated her vow, attached her girdle to the prow, and drew the ship safely into port. Her innocence was established by this prodigy.

CHAPTER XVII.

CERES—DEMETER.

Ques. Who was Ceres?

Ans. She was the daughter of Saturn and Ops, and was worshipped as the goddess of fruits and corn. It is supposed that she first invented and taught the art of tilling the earth, and sowing wheat and other grains, so that men ate wholesome bread, where before they had lived on roots and acorns.

Ques. How is Ceres represented?

Ans. As a beautiful and majestic woman, with golden hair, and crowned with ears of wheat; in her right hand she holds poppies and ears of corn, and in her left, a flaming torch.

Ques. Explain these emblems.

Ans. The hair of Ceres is golden, to represent the color of ripe corn, she holds a lighted torch, because when her daughter Proser'pine was stolen by Pluto, Ceres kindled a torch from the flames of Mount Etna, to light her on her search throughout the world. She holds a poppy, because when she was so grieved that she could neither rest nor sleep, Jupiter gave her a poppy to eat.

Ques. Relate the story of Proser'pine (Perse'phone).

Ans. None of the goddesses were willing to marry Pluto, or share his gloomy kingdom. He determined, nevertheless, to obtain a wife, even if he had to do so by violence. Proser'pine, the daughter of Jupiter and Ceres, was gathering daffodils with her companions in the plains of Enna, when Pluto suddenly appeared among them in a chariot drawn by black horses. As the maidens fled in terror, he seized Proser'pine, and striking the waters of the fountain Cy'ane with his trident, he opened a passage, through which he descended with his prize. Ceres, ignorant of what had occurred, wandered through the world in search of her daughter. At length, arriving at the fountain of Cy'ane, she perceived the girdle of Proser'pine still floating on its waters; and the nymph Arethusa informed her of what had taken place. Ceres repaired immediately to Olympus, where she made her complaint to Jupiter, and demanded that Pluto should restore her daughter. Jupiter promised to grant her request, in case Proser'pine should not have tasted food in the infernal regions. Ceres descended thither, and Proser'pine prepared joyfully to accompany her mother, when Ascal'aphus reported that he had seen her eat some seeds of pomegranate. The hopes of Ceres were thus destroyed, but Proser'pine was so indignant at the treachery of Ascal'aphus, that she changed him immediately into an owl. Jupiter endeavored to appease the resentment of Ceres by permitting Proser'pine to divide the year, spending six months with her mother on earth, the other six with Pluto in the infernal regions.

Ques. What were the most famous solemnities instituted in honor of Ceres?

Ans. The Eleusian or Eleusinian Mysteries. They were named from Eleusis, a town in Greece where they were celebrated.

Ques. What rites were practiced during these mysteries?

Ans. We cannot tell with any certainty. The penalty of death was decreed against any one who should betray the secret, or even witness the ceremonies without having been regularly initiated. Disclosures were made, however, which seem to prove that the person to be initiated was first introduced into a dark subterranean cave, where he was terrified with the most fearful sights and sounds. After this, if his courage did not fail, he was suddenly introduced into a lovely garden, and the ceremonies concluded with feasting and dancing.

Ques. Who were admitted to these rites?

Ans. Athenians only; but Hercules, to whom no one dared refuse anything, was initiated, and after him, other distinguished foreigners were admitted to what were called the Lesser Mysteries. The Athenians were eager to be admitted to these rites, because they believed that the souls of those who had not been initiated were left to wallow in mud and filth in the lower regions.

Ques. What do the early Christian writers say of these mysteries?

Ans. They speak of them as being almost as immoral as the festivals held in honor of Bacchus.

Ques. Who is said to have instituted them?

Ans. Triptol'emus, the foster-child of Ceres.

Ques. Relate the story of Triptol'emus.

Ans. When Ceres was seeking Proser'pine by sea and land, she was kindly entertained by Celeus, king of Eleusis, in Attica. She rewarded his hospitality by taking care of his young son, whom she nourished during the day with celestial food; but in the night, she covered him with fire. Under this extraordinary treatment, the infant, in a few days, became a beautiful young man. His mother, Meganira, wondered at this, and resolved to discover the cause. She watched Ceres at night, and when she saw her covering Triptol'emus with living coals, she cried out in terror, and rushed into the room to save him. Ceres punished her curiosity with death, but she adopted Triptol'emus, and sent him through the world to teach mankind the use of corn. He executed the commands of Ceres, and wherever he went, instructed men in sowing, reaping, and other arts of husbandry. Triptol'emus is usually represented as a young man, seated in a splendid chariot drawn by flying serpents.

Ques. What sacrifices were offered to Ceres?

Ans. Young heifers, swine and ears of corn wine, milk and honey were used in the libations.

Ques. What were the Ambarvalia?

Ans. They were feasts kept in the beginning of harvest, preparatory to reaping. The animal to be offered in sacrifice, was led around the fields, the husbandmen and country rustics following with shouts and songs. Virgil says of these festivities:

> Let ev'ry swain adore her power divine,
> And milk and honey mix with sparkling wine ;
> Let all the choir of clowns attend this show,
> In long procession, shouting as they go ;
> Invoking her to bless their yearly stores,
> Inviting plenty to their crowded floors.
> Thus in the spring, and thus in summer's heat,
> Before the sickles touch the rip'ning wheat,
> On Ceres call ; and let the lab'ring hind
> With oaken wreaths his hollow temples bind ;
> On Ceres let him call, and Ceres praise,
> With uncouth dances, and with country-lays.
> GEORG. I

CHAPTER XVIII.

THEMIS—ASTRÆA—NEMESIS

Ques. Who was Themis?

Ans. She instructed both gods and men, and was generally considered the goddess of law and justice. Her origin is uncertain; but she is said to have been a Titaness.

Ques. Who was Astræ'a?

Ans. She was also goddess of justice; according to some, she was the daughter of Jupiter and Themis. When the Titans took up arms against Jupiter, Astræ'a descended to earth, and mingled with the human race. This intercourse was uninterrupted during the Golden Age; in the Silver Age, Astræ'a dwelt in the mountains, and descended only amid the shades of evening, when she was unseen by men. When the Brazen Age commenced, she fled altogether from the human race, being the last among the Immortals to abandon the earth. Jupiter then changed her into the constellation Virgo, one of the signs of the zodiac. This constellation is represented by the figure of a woman holding scales in one hand, and a sword in the other. The scales have been variously explained, but they are generally supposed to be an emblem of justice. According to some, Erigo'ne, a maiden who hung herself in despair, at the death of her father, was changed into the constellation Virgo.

Ques. Who was Nem'esis?

Ans. She was the daughter of Night, and the goddess of just vengeance. It was her office to follow and punish guilty men. She had wings, but generally went on foot, which signifies that the punishment of crime, although sure, is generally slow. An ancient poet says:

> "Vengeance divine to punish sin moves slow;
> The slower is its pace, the surer is its blow."

Ques. What do you say of the temple of Nem'esis at Rhamnus?

Ans. This temple was but a short distance from the plain of Marathon. The Persians had brought with them a great block of Parian marble for the trophy which they intended to erect in honor of their expected victory. This marble fell into the hands of the Athenians, and a sculptor, said by some to have been Phidias, afterwards carved from it a beautiful statue of Nem'esis, which was placed in the temple of Rhamnus. A fragment was found in the ruins of this edifice, which is supposed to be the head of this statue; and has been presented as such to the British Museum.

CHAPTER XIX.

THE MUSES

Ques. Who were the Muses?

Ans. They were the daughters of Jupiter and Mnemo'syne, and were supposed to preside over the liberal arts and sciences.

Ques. How many Muses were there?

Ans. They were nine in number, and each presided over some particular department of literature, art or science. Their names were:

Calli'ope, who was the Muse of epic poetry, she holds in her hand a roll of parchment, or a trumpet.

Clio presided over history. She holds a half opened scroll.

Melpo'mene was the Muse of tragedy. She leans on a club, and holds a tragic mask.

Euter'pe was the patroness of music. She holds two flutes.

Er'ato inspired those who wrote of love. She plays on a nine-stringed lyre.

Terpsich'ore presided over choral dance and song. She appears dancing, and holds a seven-stringed lyre.

THE MUSES.

Ura'nia, the Muse of astronomy, holds a globe, and traces mathematical figures with a wand.

Thalia, the Muse of comedy, holds in one hand a comic mask, in the other a crooked staff.

Polyhym'nia presided over eloquence. She holds her fore-finger to her lips, or carries a scroll.

The Muses are sometimes represented as crowned with palms, and seated in the shade of an arbor, playing upon different instruments; or again, as dancing in a circle with joined hands, while Apollo is seated in their midst.

Ques. How have some writers accounted for the number of Muses?

Ans. They say that in ancient times there were but three Muses. The citizens of Sicyon employed three sculptors to execute statues of these goddesses, promising to choose from among the nine images, those which they should consider the most beautiful. When the statues were finished, they were found to be so skillfully wrought, that it was impossible to make a choice. They were all placed in the temple, and the poet Hesiod afterwards assigned them names and attributes.

Ques. What punishment did the Muses inflict on the nine daughters of Pierus, king of Æmathia?

Ans. These maidens challenged the Muses to a contest in music; they were defeated and transformed into magpies by the indignant goddesses. Tham'yris, a musician of Thrace, was struck blind for the same offence

CHAPTER XX.

Gods of the Woods, and Rural Deities.

PAN.

Ques. Who was Pan?

Ans. He was a woodland deity, and was honored by the Romans as the god of shepherds and the patron of fishing and fowling. The Latins sometimes called him Incubus or the "Nightmare," and at Rome he was worshipped as Lupercus, or Lynceus. His origin is uncertain, but he is said by some authors to have been a son of Mercury and a nymph of Arcadia.

Ques. How is Pan represented?

Ans. As half man, and half goat, having a human head ornamented with horns, and a garland of pine: he holds in one hand a crooked staff, and in the other a pipe of uneven reeds. The music which he made on this rude instrument was so sweet as to cheer the gods.

Ques. What famous action is related of Pan?

Ans. When the Gauls, under their King Brennus, made an irruption into Greece, and were about to plunder the temple of Apollo at Delphi, Pan suddenly showed himself, and so terrified them that they fled in disorder. Hence it comes that any sudden and unreasonable terror which spreads through an assemblage of persons, particularly an army, is called a panic.

Ques. What was the origin of Pan's reeds?

Ans. A beautiful nymph, named Syrinx, was so persecuted by this god, that she prayed the water-nymphs to help her, and change her into reeds, which they did. Pan saw the transformation, and was much grieved. He took some of the reeds away for a remembrance. On applying them to his lips, he found they produced the most melodious sounds, so that he formed them into a rustic pipe. Milk and honey were offered to Pan.

SATYRS AND FAUNS.

Ques. Who were these?

Ans. They were hideous monsters who dwelt in forests, and were, like Pan, half man and half goat.

TERMINUS.

Ques. Who was Terminus?

Ans. He was the god of boundaries. His statue was only a square stone, or a painted log of wood. It is probable that the Romans did not suppose Terminus to be a person, but only used the name as another term for justice, which forbids any one to trespass on another's boundaries

Landmarks and boundary stones were considered sacred by the Romans; they were crowned with garlands on festivals, offerings were laid upon them, and it was death for any one to remove one. When Constantine embraced Christianity, and placed the cross on his standard, he replaced these Terminal stones by the Christian emblem, and the custom of erecting wayside crosses, which became afterwards almost universal, is said to date from this epoch.

Terminus had a temple on the Tarpeian rock. It is said that when Tarquin the Proud wished to build a temple to Jupiter on the spot, the god of boundaries refused to give way.

VERTUMNUS.

Ques. Who was this deity?

Ans. He is generally reckoned as one of the rural divinities, and was worshipped as such by the ancient Sabines. The name comes from the Latin word verto, (to turn or change,) and was bestowed upon him in allusion to his power of taking any form he pleased. Vertumnus presided over the seasons; he was the husband of Pomona. Statues of this god were erected in every town of Italy. His festival, called Vertumnalia, was kept in October.

CHAPTER XXI.

Goddesses of the Woods.

DIANA.

Ques. Who was Diana?

Ans. She was the daughter of Jupiter and Latona, and the twin-sister of Apollo. This goddess had three names. On earth she was called Diana, and was honored as the goddess of woods and hunting; in heaven she was called Luna, and was identified with the moon, as her brother Apollo was with the sun. In hell, she was called Hec'ate, and as spirits were supposed to be subject to her, she was invoked under the latter name in all magical incantations.

Ques. What were the habits of Diana?

Ans. She shunned the society of men, and frequented the woods, attended by a train of virgins who had resolved, like her, never to marry.

Ques. Who were the attendants of Diana?

Ans. Sometimes the Ocean'ides or daughters of Ocean'us; sometimes the woodland nymphs. Diana often led a chorus of the Muses and Graces, and joined them in singing the praises of her mother Latona.

Ques. How is Diana represented?

Ans. As a very stately and beautiful woman, dressed in the garb of a huntress; she holds a bow in her hand, and a quiver of arrows is hung across her shoulders. Her feet are covered with buskins, and a bright silver crescent glitters on her forehead. Sometimes she is represented as seated in a silver chariot drawn by hounds.

Ques. Who was Chi'one?

Ans. She was a nymph beloved by Apollo. She spoke scornfully of the beauty of Diana, and the goddess, in revenge, pierced her tongue with an arrow.

Ques. Relate the story of Ni'obe.

Ans. She was the daughter of Tan'talus, and the wife of Amphi'on, king of Thebes. She was enriched with all the gifts of nature and fortune, and being made insolent by prosperity, she insulted Latona, and refused to offer incense at her shrine. Ni'obe had seven beautiful sons, and as many lovely daughters, and had boasted of their number as rendering her superior to Latona. The indignant goddess called upon Apollo and Diana to revenge the insult offered to their mother, and humble the haughty Ni'obe. This they effected by slaying, in one day, all the children of the unhappy queen. Her sons expired by the arrows of Apollo, and her daughters by those of Diana. Amphi'on killed himself in despair, and the wretched Ni'obe, widowed and childless, wept without ceasing until the pitying gods

THE NYMPHS.   89

changed her into stone. This story has furnished the subject of a very beautiful group of statuary, in which Ni'obe is represented as vainly endeavoring to shelter, beneath her mantle, the youngest and last of her children.

Ques. **Where was the** most celebrated temple of Diana?

Ans. At Ephesus in Asia Minor; it was so beautiful that it was counted among the seven wonders of the world. Two hundred and twenty years were spent in the building, although an incredible number of workmen were employed. The entire length of the temple was 425 feet, and the breadth 220; the whole was supported by 127 superb columns, each the gift of a king. The statue of the goddess was of ebony, and the most skillful painters and sculptors were employed in the decorations of the edifice.

A man named Erostratus, who was anxious to make himself famous, by whatever means, set fire to this magnificent building. This event took place on the very day on which Alexander the Great was born.

The temple was but partially destroyed, and was soon afterwards restored to its former splendor. The inhabitants of Ephesus seem to have been particularly attached to the worship of Diana. We read in the Acts of the Apostles that when they began to make converts in that city, the people were very indignant; in their zeal for their goddess they ran about the streets for the space of about two hours, crying, "Great is Diana of the Ephesians!"

This temple was despoiled by Nero, who removed many costly offerings and images, together with a large quantity of silver and gold. It was afterwards plundered by the Goths in the reign of Gallienus; and the materials of the building have been since used in the construction of other edifices. The great dome of Santa Sophia, in Constantinople, rests upon pillars of green jasper which were removed from the temple of Diana by order of Justinian.

Two pillars of the great church of Pisa were also taken from this temple, which has been so completely destroyed that the exact site is not known.

NYMPHS.

Ques. Who were the Nymphs?

Ans. They were graceful young women who attended on Diana and the greater goddesses. Some, also, had charge of certain fountains and rivers, and were called Na'iades; the nymphs of Ocean were Ne'reides and Ocean'ides. The Ore'ades were mountain nymphs, and others presided over groves and even single trees.

Ques. What were the woodland nymphs called?

Ans. Those who watched over the forests, and always lived among the trees, were called Dry'ades, from a Greek word which means an oak; the Hamadry'ades were so called because they were attached, each to some particular oak. The Hamadryad was born with the tree, flourished and died with it. This belief lingered for a long time amid the German forests, as also the superstition about water spirits.

Ques. What was the story of Arethusa?

Ans. This nymph was the daughter of Ocean'us, and an attendant of Diana. She was admired by the god of the river Alphe'us, but refuse to listen to his addresses. As she fled from his presence, he pursued. The terrified nymph had sped through all Arcadia; the shades of evening were gathering, and Alphe'us pressed close upon her fainting steps. In this extremity, Arethusa prayed to Diana for relief, and was immediately dissolved into a a fountain. Alphe'us resumed his watery form, and sought to mingle his current with hers, but Diana opened for her a passage under the sea, and she rose in the island of Ortygia, in Sicily, still followed by the stream of the Alphe'us. In proof of this fable, and of the Grecian origin of this famous fount, it was asserted that a cup which fell into the river Alphe'us in Greece, rose in the fountain of Arethusa, and that its clear waters were reddened with the blood of the victims slain at the Olympic games.

Ques. Who was Echo?

Ans. Echo was a nymph, the daughter of Air and Tellus; she was one of Juno's attendants, but offended that goddess by her talkativeness. She was so far deprived of speech, that she could only repeat the last words of every sentence which she heard. Echo loved the youth Narcissus, and seeing that he despised her affection, she pined away till nothing remained of her but her voice and bones. The latter were changed into stones, but the voice is still heard among rocks and in solitary places, repeating always the last words that are spoken.

Ques. What was the fate of Narcissus?

Ans. One legend is that he saw his image reflected in a fountain, and, not perceiving that it was but his own shadow, gazed at it, lost in admiration, until he was changed into the flower that bears his name. According to another version, Narcissus had a twin-sister who resembled him closely in form and feature, and was his constant companion. This sister died young and Narcissus, deeply lamenting her death, used to go to a neighboring fountain, and try to recall the image of his sister by gazing at his own reflection in the waters.

Ques. Were there many rural divinities?

Ans. Yes, a great number; but only a few were well known. Among those we may mention Pomona, the goddess of orchards, and Flora, the goddess of flowers. Pales was the goddess of shepherds and pastures. The Romans celebrated feasts, called Pallia, in her honor. They offered milk, and cakes of millet, that she might drive away the wolves, and prevent diseases among the cattle.

CHAPTER XXII.

Gods of the Sea.

NEPTUNE—POSEIDON

Ques. Who was Neptune?

Ans. He was the son of Saturn and Ops, and was worshipped as the god of the sea, and the father of rivers and fountains.

Ques. How is he represented?

Ans. As standing upright in a chariot made of a sea-shell; for a sceptre, he holds a trident, that is, a fork with three barbed tines; he is arrayed in a blue mantle, and is generally accompanied by his queen Amphitri'te. Neptune's chariot is drawn by sea-horses, and his attendants, who swim on either side, are human only to the waist, the body terminating like that of a fish. Whenever Neptune's chariot moved upon the waters, the sea grew calm, and tempests were appeased.

Ques. What were the offices of Neptune?

Ans. He conducted ships safely to port, and presided over horse-races.

Ques. Why was he supposed to preside over horses?

Ans. In memory of his contest with Minerva, when he produced a horse by striking on the ground with his trident. Neptune was obliged by Jupiter to aid Apollo in building the walls of Troy.

Ques. How was Neptune worshipped?

Ans. Neptune had an altar in the Circus at Rome where sacrifices were offered, and plays were acted, representing the carrying off of the Sabine women. The solemn games in honor of this god were called Consualia, and were celebrated in the month of March. While these lasted, horses were released from work, and mules were adorned with garlands.

Ques. Who were the most remarkable of Neptune's children?

Ans. Triton, and Phorcus or Proteus.

Ques. What is told of Phorcus?

Ans. He was vanquished by Atlas, and drowned in the sea; after which the people worshipped him as a god. There was another Phorcus who had three daughters, concerning whom a remarkable circumstance is related. The sisters had but one eye for their common use; each one wore it in turn, in the middle of her forehead. They were the guardians of the Gorgons, of whom Medusa was one. The hero Perseus, when about to attack Medusa, visited them, and, watching his opportunity, while one of the sisters was handing the eye to the other, he snatched it from her, and left all three in darkness.

GODS OF THE SEA.

Ques. For what was Proteus remarkable?

Ans. For his power of transforming himself instantaneously into any shape he wished.

Ques. Who was Triton?

Ans. He was the son of Neptune and Amphitri'te, and was his father's companion and trumpeter. The upper half of his body was like that of a man, but below the waist he resembled a fish; his tail was cleft and crooked, and his hair resembled wild parsley.

Ques. What other sea-monsters were celebrated?

Ans. The Sirens, also Scylla, and Charybdis.

Ques. Who were the Sirens?

Ans. They were monsters who had the faces of women, but the bodies of flying-fish; they dwelt near the promontory of Peloris, or in islands called Sirenusæ, south of Italy. By the magical sweetness of their singing, they allured all who sailed by those coasts; and after they had lulled them into a trance, drowned them in the sea.

Ques. What was there remarkable in the songs of the Sirens?

Ans. They blended the notes of different musical instruments with their voices, and adapted the style and matter of their songs to the inclination of their hearers. They had bold and stirring strains to entice the ambitious, softer melodies for the lovers of pleasure, and with still different notes, they drew on the covetous to their destruction.

Ques. Did any escape who passed those coasts?

Ans. History mentions only two; Ulys'ses and Orphe'us The first was warned against the danger by the enchantress Circe; he therefore stopped the ears of his companions with wax, and had himself firmly bound to the mast of the ship, by which means he passed the fatal coasts in safety. Or'pheus overcame them in their own art; for he sang the praises of the gods, accompanying himself upon his lyre, and made such divine melody that the music of the Sirens attracted no attention. The Fates had decreed that the Sirens should live until some one who passed by, had listened to their songs unmoved. When they saw themselves overcome by Or'pheus, they knew that their hour had come, and flung themselves headlong into the sea, where they were transformed into rocks.

Ques. Who was Circe?

Ans. She was a skillful enchantress. Having poisoned her husband, the king of the Sarmatians, she was obliged to fly into Italy, where she fixed her dwelling on the promontory Circæum. She presented to all travellers an enchanted cup; and after they had drunk, transformed them into wolves, swine or other animals. Ulys'ses escaped by throwing an herb into the cup, which rendered it powerless; he then rushed upon the sorceress with his sword, and forced her to restore his companions whom she had transformed. After this, Circe entertained Ulys'ses in a friendly manner.

Ques. What did the poets endeavor to teach by the fables of the Sirens' song, and the cup of Circe?

Ans. They wished to signify by the singing of the Sirens, the allurements of vice, and the dangers of listening to its seductions; by the story of Circe, they showed that when men drink of the cup of sensual pleasure, they become soon degraded to the level of the beasts.

Ques. Who was Scylla?

Ans. The fable relates that she was the daughter of Phorcus, and that she was transformed by the jealousy of Circe, into a frightful monster. Scylla was so much grieved by this transformation, that she cast herself into the sea, where she was changed into a rock, made famous by the many shipwrecks that occurred upon it. Over against this rock is the whirlpool of Charybdis, about which the poets relate a similar fable. They say that Charybdis was a very ravenous woman, who stole Hercules's oxen. For this theft, Jupiter struck her dead with a thunderbolt, and changed her into the whirlpool which bears her name. The ancients placed Scylla and Charybdis in the straits of Messina. It was considered a great feat to steer successfully between them.

Ques. Who was Melicertes?

Ans. He was the son of Athamas, king of Thebes, and of Ino, the daughter of Cadmus and Hermi'one. Ino offended Juno, and the goddess, in revenge, deprived Athamas of reason. The king, in his frenzy, took the queen and her children for wild beasts, and pursued them through the palace. He killed his son Learchus by dashing him against a wall, but Ino escaped, and threw herself into the sea with Melicertes in her arms. At the intercession of Venus, Neptune endowed them both with immortality. Ino became a sea-goddess under the name of Leucothea, while Melicertes was worshipped as Palæmon. He was supposed to have power in saving vessels from shipwreck, and was, therefore, invoked by mariners. The Romans called him Portunus, and honored him as the god of shores and harbors.

Ques. Who was Thetis?

Ans. She was a sea-goddess, the daughter of Nereus and Doris, and sister of the Nere'ides. She was endowed with such beauty that Jupiter himself sought her in marriage; but Prometheus, the Titan, prophesied that Thetis would give birth to a son who should be greater than his father. Jupiter thereupon desisted from his suit, and Thetis was betrothed to Peleus, king of Thessaly. Their marriage was celebrated with much pomp, all the deities of Olympus honoring the nuptial rites with their presence. Achilles, the son of Thetis, fulfilled the Titan's prophecy by his heroic exploits.

CHAPTER XXIII.

Infernal Deities.

PLUTO—HADES.

Ques. Who was Pluto?

Ans. He was the son of Saturn and Ops, and the brother of Jupiter and Neptune. In the division of his father's kingdom, the infernal regions were allotted to him, and he is therefore called the king of Hell.

Ques. How is Pluto represented?

Ans. He is seated on a throne in the midst of clouds and darkness; he wears a crown of ebony, and holds a key in his hand instead of a sceptre.

Ques. What does the key signify?

Ans. It seems to imply, that when once the dead are received into Pluto's kingdom, the gates are locked upon them and there is no escape.

Ques. What does Pluto's name signify?

Ans. The Greek name Pluto, and the Latin word Dis, signify wealth, because this god is supposed to control the hidden treasures of the earth The thunder that happens in the night time is attributed to Pluto, and he is often styled the Infernal Jupiter.

Ques. Was Pluto the same as Plutus?

Ans. No; Plutus was the god of riches, and was supposed to be the son of Jason and Ceres. He is described as being blind and lame, injudicious, and timorous.

Ques. What does this mean?

Ans. Plutus is blind and injudicious, because he passes over the virtuous to heap riches on the wicked; he is lame because riches come slowly, and timorous, because the rich watch their treasures with great fear and anxiety.

Ques. To whom was Pluto married?

Ans. As we have learned before, Pluto was married to Proser'pine, daughter of Ceres.

HELL.

Ques. How was Hell described?

Ans. The entrance to the infernal regions was by a wide, dark cave, through which the departed souls were obliged to pass; they next came to a gloomy grove, and a black lake, called Avernus; this was overhung with such poisonous vapors that no birds could fly over it. The ferryman, Charon, was always waiting on the shore to carry the dead to the other side of the lake. The ghosts of those who had not been buried with funeral rites, were obliged to wander for a hundred years by the gloomy waters of Avernus, before Charon could carry them to the other side. This superstition made the ancients very careful about burying their dead.

Ques. What do you say of the rivers of Hell?

Ans. The Styx was the most remarkable. When any of the gods swore by the Styx, the oath was sacred; if any deity was guilty of breaking such an oath, he was deprived of nectar, and excluded from the table of the gods for a year and nine days. Lethe was also a river of Hell; the name means oblivion; it is so called, because when the dead drank of its waters, they forgot all that had passed upon this earth.

Ques. What monster kept the gate of Pluto's palace.

Ans. Cer'berus; a three-headed dog, whose body was clothed with snakes instead of hair

FATES—FURIES.

Ques. Who were the Fates?

Ans. They were three sisters, the daughters of Chaos, who were appointed to watch over the thread of human life. Their names were, Clotho, Lach'esis and At'ropos; Clotho drew the thread between her fingers; Lach'esis turned the wheel, and, at the appointed moment, At'ropos cut the thread with her scissors.

Ques. Who were the Furies?

Ans. They were three sisters, Alec'to, Tisi'phone, and Megæ'ra. They are called by the poets the Daughters of Night; their office was to torment the wicked during life and after death.

Ques. How were they represented?

Ans. As hideous women with terrible countenances; they had twining serpents instead of hair, and carried snaky whips and lighted torches in their hands. They were often called by the Greeks Eumen'ides.

Ques. Of what were the Furies an emblem?

Ans. Of the evil passions of men, and the remorse which torments the wicked. When the ancients said of a man, that the Furies had taken up their abode with him, they meant that the remembrance of his crimes did not leave him any repose.

JUDGES OF THE DEAD.

Punishments inflicted on the Condemned.

Ques. Besides Pluto, who were appointed judges of the dead?

Ans. Minos, Rhadamanthus and Æ'acus. These were princes, who governed so justly during life, that the fate of the dead was entrusted to them.

Ques. What offices were assigned to each?

Ans. Rhadamanthus judged the Asiatics, Æ'acus the Europeans; and when a very difficult case arose it was referred to Minos.

Ques. Who were the most famous among the condemned?

Ans. The giants whom Jupiter conquered. Typhon was the most enormous; when he was overthrown, Jupiter was obliged to lay the whole

INFERNAL DEITIES.

Island of Sicily upon him to keep him down. Briareus was another giant, remarkable for having fifty heads and a hundred hands. According to the ancient poets, he is imprisoned under Mount Etna, and whenever he tries to move he causes terrible eruptions of the volcano. Tityus was still more cruelly punished. He was chained to the ground in the infernal regions, and such was his stature, that he covered nine acres. A frightful vulture fed continually upon his liver, which grew as fast as it was consumed, that his punishment might be eternal.

Ques. Who was Ixion?

Ans. He was the son of Phlegyas, or, according to some, of Mars. He boasted falsely that he had gained the affections of Juno. For this insolence Jupiter cast him down into hell, where he was fastened to a wheel which revolved continually.

Ques. Who was Sis'yphus?

Ans. He was a famous robber who was slain by Theseus. In hell, he was obliged to roll a huge stone up a steep mountain. When it touched the top it rolled down again, so that he was tormented with unceasing toil.

Ques. Who was Tan'talus?

Ans. He was the son of Jupiter. He invited the gods to a feast, at which he served up the flesh of his son Pelops to try their divinity. In hell he is tormented by continual hunger and thirst. He stands up to his lips in a cool fountain, whose waters recede whenever he attempts to drink. Branches laden with tempting fruit hang over him, but they are carried out of reach by a sudden gust of wind whenever he attempts to pluck them.

Ques. Who were the Beli'des?

Ans. They were fifty maidens, daughters of Dan'aus and grand-daughter of King Belus, from whom they are called. They all murdered their husbands on the wedding night, for which crime they are obliged to draw water from a deep well until they have filled an immense sieve. Their labor is therefore perpetual.

Ques. Who was Salmo'neus?

Ans. Salmo'neus was king of Elis, and was cast into hell for imitating Jupiter's thunder.

Ques. What became of the souls of good men?

Ans. After being purified from whatever slight offences they had committed in life, they were conducted to a place abounding in delights, called Elysium. When they had passed many ages in this blissful abode they returned to earth, but before doing so, they drank of the river Lethe, that they might forget the happiness they had enjoyed.

CHAPTER XXIV.

FABULOUS—MONSTERS.

Ques. Were there any fabulous monsters besides those of Hell.

Ans. Yes, many; the Centaurs, who were half man and half horse; also Geryon, who was king of the three Balearic Islands, now known as Ivica, Minorca and Majorca. For this reason, he was said to have three heads and three bodies, and passed into fable as a monster. He was probably a wicked and cruel prince. There were also the Harpies, which had the faces of women and the bodies of birds.

Ques. What was the Chimæra?

Ans. A fabulous monster, which vomited fire. It had the head and breast of a lion, the body of a goat, and the tail of a dragon.

Ques. What was intended by this fable?

Ans. Poets thus described a volcano in Lycia, on the summit of which were lions; in the middle was pasture-land frequented by goats; and the lowest part was infested by serpents. Bellerophon made this mountain inhabitable, and was therefore said to have killed the Chimæra. At present anything which is quite imaginary is called a Chimæra.

Ques. What was the Sphinx?

Ans. It was a monster with the head and shoulders of a woman, the wings of a bird, and the paws of a lion. She infested the country about Thebes, so that the people, in their distress, went to consult the oracle of Apollo. An answer was given that no remedy could be found until some one should solve the riddle that the Sphinx had proposed, and which she had learned from the Muses. The question was this: "What animal is that which goes on four feet in the morning, on two at noon, and on three in the evening?" The Thebans often met to try their skill, and when they had failed, the Sphinx carried off and devoured one of their number. At length Hæman, son of Creon, was destroyed by the monster, and the king made a public proclamation, that he would give the throne, with the hand of his sister Jocasta, to that man who should solve the riddle. Œdipus, who was then at Thebes, came forward and answered the Sphinx, that the animal was Man, because when an infant he creeps on all fours; in manhood, he walks on two feet, and when old uses a staff as a third foot. Upon hearing this answer, the Sphinx dashed her head against a rock, and expired.

Ques. Why is the story of the Sphinx interesting?

Ans. Because there still remains in Egypt an

enormous statue of the monster, carved in solid rock. Formerly, little was visible save the head and neck, but the sand which has been gathering around it for so many centuries, is now cleared away. The body is one hundred and twenty-five feet long; and the fore-paws extend about fifty feet more. The face has been much disfigured by the arrows and lances of the Arabs, who are taught by their religion to hold all images of men or animals in detestation.

Ques. What was the Phœnix?

Ans. A fabulous bird of which there never existed more than one at the same time. It excelled all other birds in beauty of plumage, and fed only on frankincense and sweet gums. When the Phœnix had attained the age of five hundred years, it built a funeral pile of odorous wood, on which it was consumed. A new Phœnix also immediately arose from the flames. The first care of the young bird was to collect the ashes of its parent, which it carried, enclosed in myrrh, to the temple of the Sun in Egypt.

CHAPTER XXV.

Household Divinities.

PENATES—LARES

Ques. What were the Pena'tes?

Ans. This name was given to a certain class of household deities, which were worshipped by the Romans in the penetralia, or innermost part of their dwellings. The greater Pena'tes governed kingdoms and provinces; others presided over cities; and the lesser Pena'tes watched over particular houses and families.

Ques. What were the Lares?

Ans. They were, according to some, the children of Mercury and the nymph Lara; they were domestic gods, and presided over houses, streets and roads. They warded off danger from without, while the Pena'tes watched over the interior of the dwelling. The spirits of ancestors sometimes watched as Lares, over the fortunes of families. This idea of the spirits of the deceased watching over their descendants, made the Romans wish to bury the dead within, or very near their dwellings. This custom was condemned by the laws of the Twelve Tables. Besides the spirit which watched over the family, each individual was supposed to have his Lar, or familiar genius, who watched over him from his birth. In early times, children were sacrificed to the goddess Mania, who was supposed by some to be the mother of the Lares. After the expulsion of the Tarquins, Junius Brutus abolished this barbarous rite, and substituted little balls of wool, and heads of garlic and poppy, in place of the human heads which had been formerly offered. The ordinary altar of the Lares was the domestic hearth; hogs, sheep and steers were among the sacrifices offered to these divinities, but the first fruits of the season were always laid upon the hearth. No family repast was properly begun, unless some portion of the viands had been first cast into the fire; in the more solemn form of marriage, the bride always threw a piece of money on the hearth, to the Lares of her family, and another on the cross roads, that they might grant her free passage to her husband's house. The Roman boy, on attaining the age of fifteen, put off his childish dress, and consecrated the golden bulla, which he had worn around his neck from infancy, to the domestic Lares.

The soldier whose term of service had expired dedicated his arms to these powerful genii; while captives, and slaves restored to freedom, hung up their fetters, in token of gratitude, by the altar of the Lares.

Ques. How were the Lares represented?

Ans. Variously; sometimes as children, sometimes as young warriors, but always accompanied by a dog.

Virtues Worshipped by the Ancients. Vices.

Ques. What Virtues were particularly honored as divinities?

Ans. The ancients not only worshipped the different Virtues, but the abstract idea of virtue itself was personified as a goddess. The Romans dedicated two temples, one to this divinity, and another, adjoining, to Honor. As the temple of Honor could only be reached by passing through that dedicated to Virtue, the votaries were reminded that it was by walking in her paths, that true honor was to be attained.

Ques. What were the emblems of Truth?

Ans. She was generally represented as a beautiful and modest virgin, with garments as white as snow. She was the daughter of Time, or Saturn, because Time always brings truth to light.

Fides, or Fidelity, had a temple near the Capitol, which was said to have been founded by Numa Pompilius. The symbols of this goddess were, a white dog, two hands joined, or sometimes two maidens with joined hands.

Ques. What were the emblems of Peace?

Ans. Pax, or Peace, was represented as a matron holding ears of corn, and crowned with olives and laurel. Her particular symbol was a caduceus, a white staff anciently borne by ambassadors when sent to treat of peace. A magnificent temple was dedicated to this goddess in the Roman Forum.

Justice was worshipped by the Egyptians, Greeks and Romans. Her emblems have been described in the article on the goddess Astræa.

Hope had a temple at Rome in the herb market. It was destroyed by lightning.

Misericordia, or Mercy, had an altar at Athens This was a public sanctuary for the unfortunate, and it was unlawful to take any one from it by force. This altar is said to have been erected by the kindred of Hercules, after the death of that hero.

Pudicitia, or Modesty, had two temples, much frequented by the Roman matrons. The second of these was founded under peculiar circumstances.

Virginia, the daughter of Aulus, a patrician of high rank, married into a plebeian family. The noble ladies of Rome were so indignant at this alliance, that they would not permit her to enter the temple of Pudicitia, nor to offer sacrifice with them. She desired to repair this public affront by some memorable action. For this purpose, she built, in the Via Longa, a temple similar to that from which she had been expelled, and dedicated it likewise to Pudicitia. Virginia then assembled the plebeian matrons, and exhorted them to honor this Virtue in such a manner, that however the patrician ladies should surpass them in power or rank, they might still excel in modest behavior and purity of life. The two temples were from that time distinguished as Pudicitia Patricia, and Pudicitia Plebeia.

Ques. Was Fortune honored as a goddess?

Ans. Yes, the ancients worshipped under this name, a certain unseen power which was supposed to exercise a supreme dominion over human affairs. Fortune had many splendid temples in Italy. Servius Tullius dedicated two at Rome; one to Bona Fortuna, the other to Fors Fortuna. This capricious goddess was sometimes represented with her eyes bandaged, her feet winged, and her right hand resting on a wheel. In the temple of Fortune at Thebes, the goddess held Wealth, represented as an infant, in her arms.

The goddess Salus, or Health, was much honored by the Romans. In ancient times, certain days in the year were set apart for her worship. Her emblems were a bowl and a serpent.

Liberty was honored as a divinity. Her emblem was the peculiar cap with which we are familiar from the representations on our own coins.

Ques. Were not the Vices also honored by the ancients?

Ans. It is certain that both the Greeks and Romans erected temples and altars to certain vices:

but it does not appear that their intention was to do them honor. In some instances, they strove to propitiate the powers of evil, that they might abstain from doing them harm. When they built a temple at Rome to Febris, or Fever, they undoubtedly wished to appease the demon or malignant deity who was supposed to send this calamity. The same superstition has been remarked among the modern Hindoos, who are said to have dedicated temples to thunder and lightning, earthquake, pestilence, etc. The Vices were always represented in such a manner as to excite abhorrence. We have an instance of this in the altar erected to Calumny at Athens.

Apelles drew an allegorical picture, in which the odious features of this Vice were strikingly portrayed. A man sits in a listening attitude, beckoning Calumny to approach. Two counsellors, Ignorance and Suspicion, stand near him. Calumny is beautiful in form and feature, but has a malignant countenance, and flashing eyes. Envy goes before, while Fraud and Conspiracy accompany her on either side. Repentance follows with woful mien and torn garments. She looks behind her, as if calling upon Truth, who is seen advancing slowly in the distance.

Discord, Fraud, etc., were represented with appropriate symbols.

CHAPTER XXVI.

Demigods and Heroes.

Ques. Who were the Demigods?

Ans. They were brave men, who had rendered themselves famous in life by illustrious actions. After their death, their countrymen believed that they were admitted among the gods, and gave them divine honors. The circumstance of a mortal taking his place among the gods, was called an Apotheosis.

Ques. Who was the most famous of the Demigods?

Ans. Hercules, the son of Jupiter and Alcmena. Juno hated him on his mother's account, and resolved upon his destruction. For this purpose she sent two monstrous serpents to kill him as he was sleeping in his cradle. The infant hero awoke, and seizing the serpents in his hands, strangled them both. Juno was not discouraged, and when Hercules was grown up, devised new means to destroy him. She persuaded Jupiter to put Hercules under the authority of Eurys'theus, king of Mycenæ, who imposed upon the hero twelve Labors, or tasks, of great danger and difficulty. Hercules was in doubt as to whether he should submit to this injustice, and consulted the oracle of Apollo at Delphi. The oracle told him that he must obey Eurys'theus, which he accordingly did. Hercules had been carefully instructed by the Centaur Chiron, and he was now equipped for his labors by the liberality of the gods. He received a sword from Mercury, a bow from Apollo, a golden breastplate from Vulcan, horses from Neptune, and a robe from Minerva.

Ques. Relate the Twelve Labors of Hercules.

Ans. They are briefly as follows:

First. He killed a terrible lion which raged in the Ne'mean forest. Hercules is usually represented as clothed in the skin of this animal, and leaning on the club which was his ordinary weapon.

Second. He destroyed the Hydra, a serpent with fifty heads, which lived in the marshes of Lerna, and ravaged the surrounding country.

Hercules noticed that where he cut off one of the heads of this serpent, two immediately sprang up. He commanded an attendant to burn the wound with a firebrand, and by this means he at length cut off the last head.

Third. He captured the savage wild boar of Mount Erymanthus, in Arcadia, and brought it bound to Eurys'theus. The tyrant was so frightened at the sight of the animal, that he shut himself up in a brazen apartment of his palace.

Fourth. He caught, after a chase which lasted an entire year, a famous stag which was sacred to Diana. It had golden horns and brazen feet.

Fifth. He killed, or drove away from Lake Stympha'lus, certain voracious birds which fed on human flesh.

Sixth. He defeated the Amazons, and obtained as a spoil, the girdle of their queen, Hippol'yte.

Seventh. Three thousand oxen had been kept thirty years in the stables of Au'geas, which had never been cleaned during the entire period. Hercules was required to perform this task, which he effected by turning the course of a river through the stables.

Eighth. He tamed the wild bull of Crete, and brought him bound to Eurys'theus.

Ninth. He overcame Diome'des, tyrant of Thrace, who fed his horses with the flesh of his guests. Hercules caused him, in turn, to serve as food to these same horses.

Tenth. He overcame Ger'yon, who had three heads and three bodies. Hercules brought into Italy the oxen of this monster, which were accustomed to feed on human flesh.

Eleventh. He killed the dragon that watched the golden apple in the garden of the Hesper'ides, and bore away the precious fruit.

Twelfth. Hercules descended alive into the infernal regions, and brought from thence the three-headed dog, Cerberus.

Ques. Did Hercules perform any other great actions?

Ans. A vast number of exploits are attributed to him. There is a plain near Narbonne, in France, covered with stones. The ancients said that Hercules was contending on this spot with two giants, when, his arrows becoming exhausted, he prayed to Jupiter for aid. The god sent down a shower of great stones, with which Hercules put the giants to flight.

Ques. Relate the death of Hercules?

Ans. This hero had slain the Centaur Nessus to revenge an insult offered to his wife, Deiani'ra. When the monster was dying, he gave Deiani'ra a charmed philter, telling her that if Hercules ever gave her cause to doubt his affection, she could secure his constancy by making him wear a garment which had been sprinkled with this potion. The credulous Deiani'ra accepted the philter, which was nothing else but the venom of the hydra which had been infused into the Centaur's blood; and it was not long before her jealousy led her to use it as she had been directed. Hercules had plundered Œchalia, and carried off, among other captives, the beautiful I'ole, daughter of the king of that city. The hero, who wished to keep a festival, and to offer sacrifice in honor of his victory, sent for a splendid robe befitting the occasion. Deiani'ra's jealousy was excited against I'ole by the reports of the messenger, and she sent her husband a tunic impregnated with the venom of the hydra. The poison soon began to work, and Hercules endeavored in vain to tear off the tunic, which clung to his flesh and consumed even the marrow of his bones. In his fury he caught the youth who had brought him the garment, by the foot, and hurled him into the sea. He then fled in his agony to the summit of Mount Œta, where he erected a funeral pyre with forest trees which he tore up by the roots. On this he laid the skin of the Ne′mean lion and his famous club, after which he ascended the pile and directed his followers to set it on fire. All refused except Philocte′tes, who pitied the sufferings of the dying hero, and obeyed his command. He received the bow and arrows of Hercules as a reward for this service. While the pyre was blazing, Jupiter sent a thunder-cloud, in which Hercules was conveyed to Olympus. Here he was endowed with immortality, and, according to some accounts, was reconciled with Juno, who gave him her daughter Hebe in marriage.

CHAPTER XXVII.

JASON.

Ques. Who was Jason?

Ans. He was the son of Æson, king of **Thessaly**, and was celebrated on account of his expedition in search of the Golden Fleece. He is also known as the husband of the famous sorceress **Mede'a**.

Ques. What was the Golden Fleece?

Ans. Phryxus, son of Athamas, king of Thebes, received from his mother a ram of a golden color, or, according to fable, with a fleece of pure gold. Some time after, Phryxus and his sister Helle, to escape from their step-mother Ino, attempted to cross the sea on this ram. Helle became terrified, and was drowned in the straits which are called from her, Hellespont. Phryxus arrived in safety at Colchis, where he sacrificed the ram to Jupiter, who placed it among the signs of the Zodiac. The fleece was hung in a grove sacred to Mars, where it was guarded by bulls who breathed flame from their nostrils, and also by a sleepless dragon. When Jason demanded his father's throne, his uncle, who wished to continue in the government, persuaded him to undertake an expedition for the recovery of the Golden Fleece. Jason, with some brave companions, among whom were Hercules, Orpheus, Castor and Pollux, went on board a ship called the Argo, from which circumstance they were called Ar'gonauts. On arriving at Colchis, they demanded the fleece, which the king, Æetes, promised to Jason on condition that he would tame the wild bulls that guarded it, kill the dragon, sow his teeth in the ground, and afterwards destroy the soldiers who should spring from them. Jason accepted the conditions, but would inevitably have perished, had not Mede'a, the king's daughter, saved him by her magical arts. Jason obtained the fleece, and fled by night from Colchis, carrying with him Mede'a, whom he married, in fulfilment of the engagement which he had made.

Ques. What else is related of Mede'a?

Ans. She lived for some time happily with Jason, upon whom she conferred an additional favor by restoring his aged and decrepit father to the vigor and beauty of youth. Jason was ungrateful for these benefits, and divorced Mede'a in order that he might marry Creüsa, the daughter of the king of Corinth.

Ques. What was Mede'a's revenge?

Ans. She murdered, in the sight of their father, the two children whom she had borne to Jason, and consumed his palace and bride in a conflagration raised by her art. As Jason was about to rush upon the sorceress, she rose in the air in a flying chariot, and escaped to Athens.

THESEUS.

Ques. Who was Theseus?

Ans. He was the son of Æ'geus, king of Athens. The Athenians were obliged to send every year, as tribute to Crete, seven of the noblest of their young men, and as many maidens. These were usually devoured by a horrible monster called Minotaur, whom Minos, the king of Crete, kept in the Labyrinth.

Ques. What was the Labyrinth?

Ans. It was a building with fifteen hundred rooms above ground, and as many underneath. These apartments had so many doors, and were connected by such intricate windings, that no one who was conducted a certain distance into the edifice, could find the entrance again.

Theseus resolved to deliver the Athenians from this dreadful tribute, and when the lots were about being cast for the fourth time, he offered himself as one of the victims. Æ'geus strove to dissuade the young hero, but in vain; and the tribute ship departed as usual under black sails, which Theseus promised his father to change for white, in case of his returning victorious.

When they arrived in Crete, the youths and maidens were exhibited before King Minos; and

Ariadne, the daughter of the king, was so much struck by the courage and generosity of Theseus that she resolved to save his life. For this purpose she gave him a ball of thread which she directed him to attach to the entrance of the Labyrinth, and to unwind as he proceeded. Theseus followed her instructions, and when he came to where the Minotaur lay, he slew him, and found his way out by the thread. The whole band then embarked for Athens.

Ques. What became of Ariadne?

Ans. She accompanied Theseus on his flight, but he was so ungrateful as to abandon her on the island of Naxos, where she had fallen asleep on the shore. Ariadne was afterwards married to Bacchus, who gave her a crown composed of seven stars, the same which we admire in the heavens as the Corona Borealis, or Northern Crown.

Ques. Of what negligence was Theseus guilty on his return to Athens?

Ans. He forgot his promise to his father with regard to the color of his sails, and Æ'geus, who watched every day for his son's return, saw the black sails in the distance. He believed from this that his son was dead. In his despair he cast himself into the sea, which was called Æge'an from his name. Theseus, after performing many other wonderful actions, was banished from his country, and died in obscurity.

CHAPTER XXVIII.

CASTOR AND POLLUX

Ques. Who were Castor and Pollux?

Ans. They were twin brothers, the sons of Jupiter and Leda. Castor was mortal like his mother, and when he died, Pollux grieved so much that Jupiter permitted him to share his immortality with his brother. It was arranged, therefore, that they should live every alternate day.

Ques. What Constellation is named from these brothers?

Ans. Gemini, or the Twins, the third sign of the Zodiac.

PROMETHEUS.

Ques. Who was Prometheus?

Ans. He was the son of Iapetus and Clymene, one of the Oceanides. He formed a man out of clay, and gave it life by means of fire which he stole from heaven.

Ques. What pretty fable is connected with this?

Ans. The poets tell us that Jupiter was so

much displeased at the theft, that he sent Pan-do'ra to Prometheus with a mysterious box, in which were imprisoned all the evils which have since afflicted the human race. Prometheus, suspecting something wrong, refused to touch the box, upon which Pando'ra carried it to his brother Epimetheus. He was less cautious, and opening the casket, set free the evils and miseries which flew abroad through the world. When he saw what he had done, he shut the box quickly, and prevented Hope, which was lying at the bottom, from escaping also. This signifies that in the midst of all human miseries, hope yet remains. The fable may have been derived from some ancient tradition of Eve's curiosity, the fall of man, and the hope left him amid so many misfortunes.

Ques. How was Prometheus punished?

Ans. Jupiter commanded Mercury to chain him to a rock on Mount Caucasus; there an eagle fed on his liver, which was continually renewed. Prometheus had, at one time, rendered Jupiter a service. The king of the gods remembered this, and permitted that after a certain time, Hercules should kill the eagle and set him free.

CHAPTER XXIX.

ORPHEUS.

Ques. Who was Orpheus?

Ans. He was the son of Apollo and the Muse Calliope. He played so sweetly on the lyre accompanying the music with his voice, that he tamed wild beasts, stayed the course of rivers, and drew the very trees to gather around him as he sung. Orpheus married the beautiful nymph Eury'dice; but on the very day of their nuptials she was stung in the foot by a venomous serpent, and died, leaving Orpheus overwhelmed with grief. Trusting to the magic of his lyre, he repaired to the infernal regions. Here, "at the music of his golden shell," the wheel of Ixion stopped; Tantalus forgot his thirst; the vulture ceased to prey on the vitals of Tityus; Cerberus fawned at the musician's feet, Proserpine was melted to tears, and the stern king of Hell was moved to pity. Eury'dice was permitted to return to the upper world, but only on condition that Orpheus did not look upon her before they passed the confines of Pluto's kingdom. Orpheus forgot this in his eagerness, and Eury'dice vanished from his sight. In his despair, he now shunned all intercourse with mankind, and retired to woods and solitary grottoes, endeavoring to forget his misfortune in the charms of music. Orpheus was murdered during the orgies of Bacchus, by the Thracian women, who were incensed at the coldness with which he had treated them. After tearing him to pieces, they threw his head into the river Hebrus, and were surprised to hear its murmur, "Eury'dice, Eury'dice!" as it was carried down the stream to the Ægean Sea. Bacchus was indignant at the cruelty of the Thracian women, and changed them into trees.

ARION.

Ques. Who was Arion?

Ans. He was a famous musician who resided at the court of Periander, king of Corinth. Impelled by a minstrel's love of wandering, he felt desirous of visiting foreign countries, and departed from Corinth, notwithstanding the earnest solicitations of Periander, who warned him in vain of the danger to which he might be exposed. After some time spent in Italy and Sicily, Arion desired to return to Corinth, and embarked for this purpose at Sarentum, taking with him the riches that he had amassed. During the voyage the mariners agreed among themselves that they would murder Arion, and seize his treasures. The unhappy musician offered in vain to abandon everything to their cupidity, if they would but spare his life. The only favor he could obtain was the choice of a grave. If he desired to be laid on shore under the green turf, they would carry his lifeless body to land, and give it sepulture. If he cared not for this, he must immediately cast himself into the sea. Arion chose the latter alternative, but begged that he might die as became a bard, after having played for the last time upon his lyre, and sung his own death-song. The mariners granted his request, not from pity, but they desired to hear so famous a minstrel; music had charms even for their rude hearts.

Arion attired himself in festal robes; his mantle was of purple fringed with gold, and his brow was adorned with a golden wreath. He struck his lyre with the ivory wand, and sung a sweet and mournful melody. Then, commending himself to the friendly Nereides, he sprang into the sea. The waves closed above him, and the ship held on its way. The inhabitants of the deep had gathered around as Arion sung, and now, as he was struggling in the waves, a dolphin took him on his back, and carried him safe to shore. Periander received his friend with a cordial welcome, and listened with wonder to the story of his escape. When the ship arrived, he ordered the mariners to be brought before him, and inquired if they knew anything of Arion

They replied confidently that they had left him well and happy at Sarentum. Upon this Arion stepped forth, clothed in gold and purple, and holding his lyre as when he had cast himself into the sea. Overcome with terror, the guilty men confessed their crime, and suffered the punishment they had so well deserved. This event was commemorated by a statue of brass which was consecrated at Tænarus. It represented a man mounted on a dolphin.

AMPHION.

Ques. Who was Amphi'on?

Ans. He was the son of Anti'ope and Jupiter. He obtained the kingdom of Thebes, which he governed conjointly with his twin-brother Zethus. Amphi'on cultivated the art of music; he was instructed by Mercury, who gave him a golden lyre with which he is said to have built the walls of Thebes, causing the stones to move and place themselves in order, as he played. Amphi'on married Ni'obe, and became the father of seven sons and as many daughters, who were all slain by Apollo and Diana. He is said to have killed himself in despair. The legend of the building of the walls of Thebes, is probably an allusion to the old Dorian and Æolian custom of erecting the walls of cities with public solemnities, and to the sound of musical instruments.

CHAPTER XXX.

ATLAS.

Ques. Who was Atlas?

Ans. He was a king of Mauritania, the son of the Titan Jap'etus, and the nymph Clym'ene; he was, therefore, brother of Prometheus. He is represented as sustaining the heavens on his shoulders. Atlas had been warned that he would suffer much from a son of Jupiter. When Perseus was returning from the conquest of the Gorgons, he arrived in the dominions of Atlas, of whom he claimed the rites of hospitality, declaring at the same time his divine parentage. The king, remembering the prophecy with regard to Jupiter's offspring, repulsed him harshly. This conduct brought upon Atlas the calamity which he feared; for Perseus, indignant at so much inhumanity, showed him the head of Medusa, and changed him into the mountain which bears his name.

The fable, that Atlas sustained the heavens on his shoulders, has been explained by saying he was an astronomer, who observed the motion of the heavenly bodies from the summit of a lofty mountain, to which his name was afterwards given.

Ques. Who were the children of Atlas?

Ans. By his wife Peli'one, he had seven daughters, who were called Pleiades; they were changed into stars, and form the beautiful group which we admire in the constellation Taurus. Atlas had seven other daughters who underwent the same transformation; they were placed in the head of Taurus, and were called by the Greeks, Hyades, from a word which signifies " to rain."

The Hesperides, or Western Maidens, were three celebrated nymphs, concerning whose parentage ancient writers are not agreed. Hesiod speaks of them as the daughters of Night, but according to others, they were the offspring of Atlas and Hesperis. At the bridal of Jupiter and Juno, the different deities brought nuptial presents; among these, Juno most admired some branches loaded with golden apples, which were offered by the goddess of the Earth. She begged the Earth to plant them in her gardens, which extended as far as Mount Atlas. The Hesperides were directed to watch these trees, but they proved unfaithful, and frequently plucked the apples for themselves. Juno sent, therefore, a terrible dragon to guard the precious fruit. This monster was the offspring of Typhon, and had a hundred heads, so that it never slept.

ORION.

Ques. Who was Ori'on?

Ans. His origin is doubtful; according to some writers, he was the son of Neptune and Eury'ale. The accounts given of his exploits and of his death are many and contradictory. According to one legend, Ori'on was a famous hunter; having boasted that he could subdue the wildest and fiercest animals, the earth was displeased at his presumption, and sent a scorpion to sting him. The hero was changed, after death, into a constellation which is known as the most resplendent group in the winter heavens.

PERSEUS.

Ques. Who was Perseus?

Ans. He was the son of Jupiter, and of Danaë, the only daughter of Acrisius, king of Argos. This prince had been warned by an oracle that his daughter would have a son, who was destined to deprive him of life. Acrisius resolved, in consequence, that Danaë should never marry. To guard against the possibility of such an event, he imprisoned her in a brazen apartment which he had diligently guarded.

Jupiter had seen and admired the young princess, and he now found means to visit her by transforming himself into a shower of gold, which we may take for a poetical manner of saying that he bribed the guards. When Acrisius discovered that his precautions had been of no avail, he enclosed Danaë and her infant son in a coffer, which he cast into the sea. The coffer was carried by the waves to the island of Seriphus, where a fisherman named Dictys drew it ashore in his net. He was much surprised at beholding Danaë and the infant Perseus, and brought them immediately to Polydectes, who reigned in that island. Polydectes received the strangers kindly, but when Perseus was grown, he strove to effect his destruction by engaging him in an expedition against the Gorgons. This adventure has been already related, in the article on Minerva. It was followed by the rescue of Androm eda, which is too remarkable to be omitted.

Ques. Who was Androm'eda?

Ans. She was the daughter of Cepheus, king of Ethiopia. Her mother, Cassiopeia, had boasted that she was fairer than Juno and the Nereides. The offended nymphs complained to Neptune, who sent a sea-monster to ravage the dominions of Cepheus. The people, in their distress, had recourse to the oracle of Jupiter Ammon, but the god declared that the country could not be freed from this calamity, unless Androm'eda were given up to be devoured by the monster. Cepheus consented to the sacrifice, and his daughter was chained to a rock by the sea-shore, where she was abandoned to her fate.

Perseus, returning through the air, from his conquest of the Gorgons, saw the unhappy maiden and resolved to rescue her. He asked her hand as his only reward, which Cepheus readily promised.

When the sea-monster appeared, Perseus showed him the head of Medusa, and changed him into a rock, which was long famous upon that coast. Phineus, who had been betrothed to Androm'eda, opposed her marriage with Perseus, and changed the nuptial solemnities into a scene of discord and bloodshed.

The head of the Gorgon again procured for Perseus an easy victory. He warned his friends to avert their eyes, and displayed the frightful trophy, upon which Phineus and his followers were changed into stone, in the very attitudes in which they fought.

Polydectes, who had persecuted Danaë in the absence of Perseus, was punished in the same manner. The hero afterwards fulfilled the oracle by killing his grandfather, whom he did not know, by an accidental blow of a quoit.

Perseus, Androm'eda, Cepheus, and Cassiopeia were changed, after death, into the constellations which bear their names.

CHAPTER XXXI.

BELLEROPHON

Ques. Who was Beller'ophon?

Ans This hero was the son of Glaucus, and grandson of Sis'yphus, king of Corinth. Having accidentally killed one of his relatives, he fled, as was usual in such circumstances, and was received with much kindness by Prœtus, king of Argos. Beller'ophon had not, however, been long at Argos when the king was prejudiced by a calumnious report, and became jealous of the young hero. As he was ashamed to violate the rights of hospitality, he despatched Beller'ophon to his father-in-law, Joba'tes, king of the Lycians, with sealed letters in which he requested that prince to put the bearer to death. Joba'tes was also unwilling to imbrue his hands openly in the blood of a guest; he resolved, therefore, to effect his purpose indirectly, by engaging Beller'ophon in dangerous enterprises.

The first task imposed upon the hero, was the slaying of the Chimæra, a fabulous monster which we have already described, and which was then

Demigods and Heroes. 135

spreading terror through the kingdom of Lycia. Before proceeding to the combat, Beller'ophon took counsel of the soothsayer, Polyi'dus, who advised him to procure, if possible, the winged steed Peg'asus. For this purpose, he directed him to pass the night in the temple of Minerva. There the goddess visited him in a dream, and gave him a golden bridle, instructing him as to its use. On awaking, Beller'ophon found the bridle in his hand, and repaired immediately to the spring at which Peg'asus was accustomed to drink. The winged steed submitted to the golden bit, Beller'ophon mounted him fearlessly, and was borne through the air to his combat with the Chimæra. When he returned to Joba'tes with the spoils of the monster, the king sent him to fight against certain people, called Sol'ymi, whom he had much difficulty in subduing. He next defeated the Amazons, a nation of female warriors, and destroyed a party of Lycians, who laid an ambush for him on his return. Joba'tes perceived from these exploits that his guest was indeed allied to the gods, and abandoned all further designs against him. He even gave him his daughter in marriage, and declared him his successor in the kingdom.

Beller'ophon might have ended his days in happiness and prosperity, had he not irritated the gods by his pride. He conceived the project of mounting to heaven on his winged steed; Jupiter was indignant, and sent a gad-fly which stung the horse, and caused him to throw the presumptuous rider. Beller'ophon, lame and blind from his fall, wandered in lonely places, avoiding the haunts of men, until death came to relieve his misery.

DEUCALION.

Ques. Who was Deucalion?

Ans. He was king of Thessaly, and son of Prometheus. During his reign, there occurred so great a flood that the whole earth was covered with the waters. Of the entire human race, only Deucalion and his wife, Pyrrha, were saved. When the waters abated, the ship in which they were carried rested upon Mount Parnassus, and they consulted the oracle of Themis, to know by what means the earth might again be peopled. The oracle directed that they should cast behind them the bones of their Great Mother. Understanding by this expression the earth, which is the common mother of all, they gathered stones which they cast behind them, as they had been commanded, when a great prodigy ensued. The stones thrown by Deucalion assumed human form and became men, and those thrown by Pyrrha were changed into women.

Ques. How is this fable explained?

Ans. It is supposed that Deucalion and Pyrrha were remarkable for their piety and virtue; and that by precept and example, they subdued the ferocity of their subjects. In this manner they softened those who before were hard like stones, so that gentleness and humanity began to reign among them.

DÆDALUS.

Ques. Who was Dæd'alus?

Ans. He is said to have been a native of Athens, eminent for his skill in architecture and statuary. His nephew Perdix wrought with him, and showed much inventive genius. Having observed the teeth of a serpent, or, according to some, the backbone of a fish, Perdix invented the carpenter's saw, and applied it to the cutting of timber. By this and other efforts of skill, the young man excited the jealousy of Dæd'alus, who killed him by casting him down from the summit of the Acropolis. Perdix was transformed into a partridge, a timid bird which seems still mindful of its fall, and keeps to low coverts, avoiding high places and lofty flights. For this murder, Dæd'alus was sentenced to banishment by the Court of the Areop'agus. He found an asylum with Minos, king of Crete, for whom he constructed the famous Labyrinth. Having incurred the displeasure of Minos, Dæd'alus was imprisoned in a lofty tower. As there seemed no other means of escape, he resolved on attempting a flight through the air. For this purpose, he made wings for himself and his son Ic'arus, which were so skilfully contrived, that, by their aid, they mounted boldly in the air, and directed their flight over the sea. Icarus disregarded his father's instructions, and approached so near the sun that its heat melted the wax which united the feathers of his wings. He could no longer sustain himself, and was drowned in that sea which is called Icarian, from his name. Dæd'alus arrived in Sicily, where he was employed by Coc'alus, king of that island, in the erection of many splendid edifices.

Various explanations have been given of the fable of Dæd'alus. The most probable opinion is that there really existed an architect of that name, whose fame was such that all the improvements made in those early times in architecture and sculpture were attributed to him by popular tradition. He introduced the use of masts and sails in ships, and he is said to have been the first who represented statues in natural and lifelike attitudes, and with open eyes. Dæd'alus is also mentioned as the inventor of the axe, plumb-line and augur.

CEYX—HALCYONE—THE HALCYON BIRDS.

Ques. Who was Ceyx?

Ans. He was a king of Trachinia, who married Halcy'one, a daughter of the god Æolus. Ceyx was drowned on his way to consult the oracle of Claros. Halcy'one was apprised of the sad event in a dream, in which she saw her husband stand before her, with pallid countenance and dripping garments. She hastened to the strand at break of day, and gazing over the waters, beheld the body of Ceyx borne towards her by the waves. In her despair, she cast herself into the sea, but the gods took pity on the faithful pair, and transformed them into halcyons. According to the poets, it was decreed that the sea should remain calm while these birds built their nests upon it. Notwithstanding the querulous, lamenting note of the halcyon, it was regarded by the ancients as a symbol of tranquillity, and as it seemed to make its home upon the waters, it was consecrated to Thetis. Pliny tells us that these birds constructed their floating nests during the seven days immediately preceding the winter solstice, and laid their eggs in the seven days succeeding. These are the "halcyon days" of antiquity, and this expression is still used to denote a period of bright and tranquil happiness.

The only bird of modern times which at all resembles the halcyon described by Pliny and Aristotle, is the *Alcedo Ispida*, a species of martin called by the French, martin-pêcheur. This martin, however, makes its nest on shore, lays its eggs in the spring, and has no connection with calm weather. The large sponge-like ball which was taken by the ancients for the floating nest of the halcyon, was in reality a zoöphyte, of the class named by Linnæus, halcyonium.

CHAPTER XXXII.

MELEAGER—THE CALYDONIAN HUNT

Ques. What was the story of this prince?

Ans. Meleager was the son of Œneus and Althea, king and queen of Calydon. After his birth, the Fates entered the chamber of Althea, and foretold that the life of the child should expire with a billet of wood then burning on the hearth. Althea immediately seized and quenched the brand, which she secured in an oaken chest. Meleager had already attained the years of manhood when he took part in the expedition generally known as the Calydonian hunt. Œneus had, upon one occasion, in offering sacrifice to the gods, neglected the honors due to Diana, and the goddess, in revenge, sent a wild boar of enormous size to lay waste the fields of Calydon. The boldest hunters feared to attack the monster, whose eyes shone with fire, while its bristles stood erect like spears, and its tusks resembled those of an Indian elephant. The cornfields and vineyards were trampled down in its path, and the terrified husbandmen everywhere fled in dismay. At length Meleager called on the heroes of Greece to join in a hunt and destroy the common foe

The Calydonian Hunt.

There came on the appointed day, Castor and Pollux, Theseus and his friend Pirothous, Peleus, afterwards father of Achilles, Telamon, father of Ajax, Nestor, then a youth, and many others of heroic fame. All eyes were, however, attracted by the fair huntress Atalanta. Her girdle was of burnished gold, an ivory quiver hung from her shoulder, and she carried a bow in her left hand.

They soon reached the monster's lair. Roused by the baying hounds, he rushed forth, trampling down and slaying the nearest huntsmen. In vain Jason threw his spear, praying that Diana might guide his arm. It glanced aside, and the weapon of Telamon proved equally harmless, while Nestor was obliged to seek safety in the branches of a tree. The first wound was inflicted by an arrow from the bow of Atalanta. Meleager, following up this advantage, despatched the monster with his spear. The heroes crowded around to congratulate the victor, who offered the head of the boar and the bristling hide to Atalanta. The huntress accepted the trophies, but the uncles of Meleager, indignant that a woman should bear off the honors of the day, snatched them rudely from her. Meleager forgot, in his anger, the ties of kindred, and slew the offenders on the spot.

As Althea was going to the temple to return thanks for her son's victory she beheld the bodies of her murdered brothers. When she learned that they had fallen by the hand of Meleager, the Furies took possession of her soul. Entering hastily into the palace, she snatched the fatal brand, so long preserved, and cast it into the flames. At the same moment Meleager started with sudden pain, his strength ebbed away, and as the brand fell to ashes, the soul of the hero was breathed forth on the light winds.

When the deed was accomplished Althea killed herself in despair. The sisters of Meleager wept his loss, until Diana, pitying their sorrow, changed them into birds called Meleagrides.

NISUS AND SCYLLA.

Ques. Relate the story of their transformation?

Ans. Nisus was king of Megara; this city was closely besieged by Minos, but all his efforts were vain, as the Fates had decreed that it should not be taken, so long as a purple lock which grew on the head of Nisus, remained uncut. Scylla, the daughter of this prince, admired the majestic person of Minos, and the valor which he displayed. Believing that he would reward her treachery by making her his queen, she cut the fatal lock while her father slept. Minos received the gift with horror, and, when the city was taken, refused to permit Scylla to accompany him to Crete. In despair, she clung to the prow of his ship; but Nisus, who had just been transformed into a hawk, swooped down upon her from the sky. Scylla cast herself into the sea, and was transformed at the same moment into a lark.

ERISICHTHON

Ques. Who was Erisichthon?

Ans. He was a profane person and a despiser of the gods. There stood in a grove sacred to Ceres, a stately oak which overtopped the trees around as they did the garden shrubs. Erisichthon commanded his attendants to fell the tree, and when they hesitated, he snatched an axe himself, and struck the sacred wood. Blood flowed from the wounded trunk, and a voice from the Dryad dwelling in the oak, warned him of the punishment which awaited his impiety. Erisichthon persisted in his crime, and at length the tree, severed by repeated blows, and drawn with ropes, sunk to the ground, prostrating half the grove in its fall. The indignant Dryades went to Ceres in mourning garb, and invoked vengeance on the head of their impious foe. The goddess was moved, and delivered Erisichthon into the power of Famine. As the Fates had decreed that this goddess and Ceres should never meet, an Oread was sent to the ice-clad plains of Scythia, where Famine chiefly dwelt. Arriving at Mount Caucasus, the nymph found her in a stony field, tearing up with teeth and claws the scanty herbage. The pale goddess obeyed the command of Ceres, and visiting the dwelling of Erisichthon, she breathed upon him as he slept. Awaking he craved food, but the more he consumed, the more his hunger raged. In vain the unhappy man spent all his substance to obtain relief; he was reduced to misery and famished as before. He had one daughter called Mestra, an only child, whom he sold to procure food. The maiden scorned to be a slave, and standing with her purchaser on the sea-shore, she lifted her hands, and invoked the aid of Neptune. The god immediately changed her form, so that she appeared to be an aged fisherman mending nets.

The master, strangely surprised at the sudden disappearance of his slave, questioned the supposed fisherman. Mestra replied that she had seen no one, and he proceeded to search for the fugitive elsewhere. She then resumed her own form, and returned to her father, who was well pleased to find that he had still both his daughter and the money for which he had sold her. He again resorted to this base expedient, but as often as Mestra was sold, she was transformed, by the favor of Neptune, now into a horse, now an ox, and now a stag; and so escaped from her purchaser.

All means proved insufficient to supply the wants of the unhappy Erisichthon, who was compelled by hunger to devour his own flesh before death came to end his misery.

CHAPTER XXXIII.

Poets of Classic Fable.

HOMER—HESIOD—VIRGIL—OVID.

Ques. Who was Homer?

Ans. Everything relating to this poet is involved in obscurity. The two biographies of him which were formerly attributed to Herodotus and Plutarch, are evidently fabulous; their real authors are not known. Nothing is known certainly regarding Homer's parentage, his birth-place, or even the exact era in which he lived. Seven cities contended for the honor of having given this great poet to the world; these were Smyrna, Chios, Col'ophon Sal'amis, Rhodes, Argos and Athens.

Smyrna appears to have the best claim, and it is considered certain that the poet was by birth an Ionian; the Ionic is the dialect employed in his works, with a slight mixture, however, of the Æolic, and other forms. With regard to the time in which Homer lived, there is much difference of opinion among the learned, some placing him in the ninth, others in the tenth century before our era. The latter opinion is the more probable.

According to the account generally given, Homer was for many years a schoolmaster in Smyrna. He afterwards abandoned this occupation, and spent some time in travelling.

He made several voyages in the company of a sea captain named Mentes; but at length his sight became so much affected that he was obliged to remain on shore at Ithaca. While in this island, he was kindly entertained by a wealthy man named Mentor, who related to him the traditionary tales on which he afterwards founded the Odyssey.

Becoming totally blind, Homer returned to Smyrna, where he probably composed the greater part of his poems. He afterwards led a wandering life, gaining wealth and fame by the recitation of his verses. He died at Ios, one of the Cyclades, where he was buried. The fame of Homer is founded on his two great poems, the Iliad and the Odyssey. The first of these has been always considered among the finest productions of human genius. Homer is distinguished not only for his sublimity, but for the high moral tone which pervades his works.

Ques. Who was Hesiod?

Ans. This poet flourished about half a century later than Homer. He was a Bœotian, and in his youth tended sheep upon Mount Helicon. He emigrated afterwards to Orchomenos, in western Bœotia, where he **died.**

MYTHOLOGY. 147

The only complete works of Hesiod now extant are the " Works and Days," and the Theogony, or " Birth of the Gods." The latter work consists of a long and rather tedious catalogue of the gods and goddesses; it is valued as containing an accurate account of the Grecian deities. The description of the Battle of the Titans and the Gods, at the close of the work, is considered one of the most sublime passages in classic poetry; Milton has borrowed from it in his Battle of the Angels.

Ques. When did Virgil flourish?

Ans. Publius Virgilius Maro, was born near Mantua in the year 70, B. C. He received a liberal education, and inherited from his father a considerable estate. Of this he was deprived during the civil troubles which distracted Italy, but it was afterwards restored at the intercession of a powerful friend. His gratitude towards this kind benefactor, and the happiness felt by the poet in the peaceful possession of his patrimony, form the subject of his first pastoral poem or Eclogue. Virgil enjoyed the favor of Augustus, with the friendship of Mæcenas and other generous and powerful patrons; his life was, therefore, spent in ease and prosperity. He died at Brundusium, in the year 19, B. C.

The Eclogues, sometimes called also Bucolica or Bucolics, are ten short pastoral poems. The fourth, entitled Pollio, has given rise to much speculation on account of its striking coincidence with Scripture. Many suppose that the poet was acquainted with the prophecies of Isaiah.

The Georgics treat of agriculture, the care of cattle, the raising of bees, etc. These peaceful arts had been much neglected in Italy during the civil wars; Virgil hoped to revive the taste for rural pursuits, by his beautiful descriptions of country life. The Æneid, the last and greatest of his works, is an epic poem in twelve books. It is a history of the wanderings of Æneas, and the settlement of the Trojans in Italy.

Virgil is considered inferior to Homer in sublimity, but he exceeds him in sweetness and in the beauty of his descriptions. The moral, and even to a certain extent the religious spirit which pervades his writings is beyond praise, and places him almost alone among the poets of antiquity.

Ques. When did Ovid write?

Ans. Ovidius Naso was born in the year 43, B. C., at Sulmo (now Sulmona), a town about ninety miles distant from Rome. The date of his birth is rendered memorable in history by the murder of the great Cicero. Ovid belonged to an equestrian family; he was educated at Rome, and enjoyed every advantage that splendid capital afforded. He showed his taste for poetry at an early age, but was dissuaded from cultivating this art by his father, who wished him to apply exclusively to the study of eloquence. Ovid gained some distinction as an orator; but when the death of his elder brother left him sole heir to an ample fortune, his natural inclination prevailed, and he gave himself up to literary pursuits. A career of unexampled prosperity was now opened to the poet. He enjoyed the favor of Augustus, and the friendship of the most distinguished men in Rome; his verses were universally admired, they were sung in the streets and at entertainments, or were recited in the theatre amid bursts of applause. Ovid was not content with the nobler pleasures of fame and friendship, but plunged without restraint into all the vices and follies of which the Roman capital was the centre. This career of prosperity and pleasure was brought suddenly to a close. Ovid was banished by Augustus to Tomi, (now Temiswar) on the shores of the Euxine.

The decree was executed with the utmost severity. But one wretched night was allowed to the poet to deplore his fate, and take leave of his friends. His wife begged in vain to be allowed to accompany her husband in his exile. It is not known by what crime the unfortunate poet merited so severe a punishment. The immoral tendency of some of his poems, was the ostensible reason set forth by the emperor; but these verses had been written many years before. It is evident, therefore, that he must have offended Augustus in some manner which the latter did not choose to make public. Ovid wrote, in his exile, poems appropriately named "Tristia," in which he bewails his hard fate, and describes the scenes by which he was surrounded. From the severity of the climate, and the inroads of the barbarians, the fields were without grain, the hills without vines; no stately oaks clothed the mountain-side, no willows drooped along the banks; a scanty growth of wormwood alone covered the desolate plains. Spring brought with it neither birds nor flowers. In Summer, the sun was obscured by clouds; the Autumn shed no fruits, but through every season of the year, the wintry winds blew with prodigious violence, and lashed the waves of the boisterous Euxine on its desert shore. The only animated object was the wild Sarmatian driving his car, yoked with oxen, across the icy waste, himself wrapped in furs, his shaggy hair and beard sparkling with the hoar frost and flakes of snow. Such was the abode for which the poet was compelled to exchange the theatres, the porticoes and gardens of Rome, the court of Augustus, and the sunny skies of Italy. He died in the ninth year of his exile, and the sixty-first of his age.

The poems of Ovid, however beautiful otherwise, are all more or less objectionable on account of their immoral tendency; the corruption of the author's private character has left its impress on all his works.

The claim of Ovid to be numbered among the poets of mythology, rests chiefly on his Metamorphoses. This is a collection of legends of all the transformations said to have taken place in heathen mythology, beginning with the earliest times, and closing with the changing of Julius Cæsar into a star. The stories are not themselves original; they are principally Greek and Oriental fictions, interspersed, perhaps, with a few Latin or Etruscan fables. There are, in all, two hundred and fifty of these stories. Ovid was engaged in correcting this, his greatest work, when he was surprised by the sentence of banishment. In a fit of impatience and despair, he threw it into the flames. Some of his friends possessed copies, and the poem was thus preserved.

If the Metamorphoses had been destroyed by this rash act, we would have lost many interesting fables which have been rendered immortal by the beauty of Ovid's verse and his graceful fancy.

The Tristia are not so generally admired They turn principally on the poet's personal misfortunes; and this subject, however absorbing to himself, soon becomes wearisome to the reader. Ovid composed a poem in the harsh dialect spoken by the Getæ who dwelt on the borders of the Euxine Sea. The barbarians listened with delight to his recitations, until their anger was excited by his constant complaints of their rude manners and inhospitable climate.

CHAPTER XXXIV.

Heroes Celebrated by the Poets.

AGAMEMNON.

Ques. Who was Agamemnon?

Ans. He was king of Mycenæ, and commander-in-chief of the Grecian forces during the siege of Troy. The combined fleet was detained for a long time at Aulis, owing to the wrath of Diana, whom Agamemnon had offended by killing one of her favorite deer. Calchas, the soothsayer, was consulted; he declared that the goddess could only be appeased by the sacrifice of Iphige'nia, the oldest daughter of the monarch. She was accordingly led to the altar, but Diana was moved with pity, and carried the maiden with her to Tauris, leaving a hind in her place. The quarrel of Agamemnon with Achil'les, and the troubles that resulted, form the principal subject of Homer's Iliad. In the division of captives, after the taking of Troy, Cassandra, one of the daughters of Priam, fell to the lot of Agamemnon. This princess had been endowed by Apollo with the gift of prophecy, but as she refused afterwards to listen to the suit of that god, he decreed that no one should attach any credit to her predictions. It was so in the present instance. Clytemnestra, the queen of Agamemnon, believing, and perhaps hoping, that her husband would not return, had given a promise of marriage to Ægisthus, who already considered himself king of Mycenæ. Cassandra warned Agamemnon against returning thither, but her prediction was disregarded. Agamemnon was assassinated immediately on his arrival at Mycenæ; according to the tragic poets, it was Clytemnestra who dealt the fatal blow.

ACHILLES.

Ques. Who was Achil'les?

Ans. He was the son of Peleus, king of Phthio'tis in Thessaly; his mother was Thetis, a sea-goddess. Many incredible stories are told concerning the manner in which the hero was nursed in his infancy. According to one account, his mother designed to make him immortal, and for that purpose anointed him with ambrosia during the day, and laid him in the fire at night. The fears of Peleus interrupted this strange treatment, and Achil'les remained subject to death. Calchas had declared that Troy could not be taken without his aid, and Thetis, who was aware that her son was destined to perish if he joined the expedition, disguised him in female attire, and concealed him among the daughters of King Lycome'des. Ulys ses was sent to discover his retreat, which he effected by the following stratagem. Attired as a travelling merchant, he presented himself at court, and displayed before the queen and her maidens, various articles of female attire. Some pieces of armor were disposed among the merchandise; by the order of Ulys'ses, a trumpet was suddenly blown, when the disguised Achil'les betrayed himself by seizing the armor. The young warrior was then obliged to join the expedition. During the siege, Achil'les had a dispute with Agamemnon, concerning some female captives; considering himself wronged, he withdrew from the contest, and no entreaties could induce him to return to the field. The death of his friend Patroclus, who fell by the hand of Hector, at length aroused him to action. Achil'les' armor, which he had lent to Patroclus, had become the spoil of Hector, and it was upon this occasion that Vulcan fabricated for the hero, the famous suit which is described in the Iliad. Arrayed in this Achil'les performed prodigies of valor, and at length killed Hector, after a desperate combat. According to Homer, Achil'les took an ignoble revenge on the dead body of his foe, which he dragged at his chariot-wheels, three times around the tomb of Patroclus. The corpse of the Trojan hero was yielded at last, to the tears and supplications of Priam, and a truce was granted to the Trojans, for the performance of the funeral rites. Achil'les was himself slain soon after; his ashes were mingled in a golden urn with those of Patroclus, and a tomb was erected to both heroes, on the promontory of Sigœum.

The vindictive spirit of Achil'les knew no repose, even in death. After the fall of Troy, his ghost appeared to the Greeks, and commanded them, with fearful menaces in case of refusal, to sacrifice on his tomb, Polyxena, one of the daughters of Priam. The unhappy maiden was torn from her mother's arms, and immolated by Pyrrhus, the son of Achil'les. Hec'uba learned soon after the sad fate of her son Polydorus. This young prince, who had been commended by Priam to the care of Polymnestor, king of Thrace, was treacherously murdered by that monarch. The bereaved mother planned a terrible revenge. Promising disclosures with regard to hidden treasures, she induced Polymnestor and his children to visit her in secret. Then, aided by her fellow captives, Hec'uba murdered the young princes and put out the father's eyes. While endeavoring to escape from the vengeance of the Thracians, she was suddenly transformed into a dog.

CHAPTER XXXV.

ULYSSES.

Ques. Who was Ulys'ses?

Ans. He was king of Ithaca, and had been, like many other princes of Greece, a suitor of the beautiful Helen. Believing that he had no hope for success among so many competitors, Ulys'ses asked the hand of Penel'ope, daughter of Icarus. His suit was granted; but when he was about to depart with his bride, Icarus was so much grieved, that he tried to persuade Penel'ope to remain with him, and not accompany her husband to Ithaca. Ulys'ses bade her act according to her inclination. saying that she was free to remain, if such was her desire. Penel'ope made no reply, but dropped her veil over her face. Icarus urged her no longer, and when she was gone, he erected a statue to Modesty, on the spot where they parted. When the Grecian princes were called upon to revenge the abduction of Helen, Ulys'ses was unwilling to leave his peaceful kingdom, and sacrifice the happiness he enjoyed in the company of

Penel'ope. Hearing that Palame'des had come to summon him to the field, he pretended to be insane. He yoked a horse and a bull together, and began ploughing the sands of the sea-shore, sowing salt instead of grain. Palame'des caused Telem'achus, the infant son of Ulys'ses, to be laid before the plough, and the manner in which the father hastened to remove the child, convinced every one that his insanity was feigned. He was obliged, therefore, to join the expedition against Troy, but he never forgave Palame'des for having exposed his stratagem. The manner in which Ulys'ses revenged himself is not calculated to give us a very high opinion of the hero. During the siege, he brought forward a false accusation against Palame'des, which he supported so well, that the latter was condemned, and put to death.

Ulys'ses distinguished himself during the war, by his wisdom and prudence in council, and his courage on the field of battle. We have already spoken of the part which he took in carrying off the Palladium of Troy. As a reward for his services, he received the armor of Achil'les, which Ajax had disputed with him.

After the fall of Troy, Ulys'ses embarked with the intention of returning to Greece, but he met with so many extraordinary adventures, that it was only after ten years of peril and hardships, that he was permitted to land upon the shores of Ithaca.

The Odyssey, the second of the two great poems

attributed to Homer, is a history of the wanderings of Ulys'ses. After some adventures of minor importance, the ships of the hero were overtaken by a storm which drove them southward for nine days, and as many nights, until they reached the country of the Lotus-eaters. When the tempest abated, Ulys'ses sent some of his companions on shore. They were kindly entertained by the Lotus-eaters, who regaled them with their own favorite food, the lotus plant. This was of such a nature, that all who partook of it forgot home and friends, and were filled with a sort of indolent contentment, so that they had no other desire than to remain always in that country. Ulys'ses was obliged to have these men dragged away by force, and even then, it was necessary to bind them with ropes to the benches of the ship.

The escape of Ulys'ses from the cavern of the Cyclops and from the enchantments of Circe has been already related. After passing safely between Scylla and Charybdis, Ulys'ses landed in the island of Thrinakia, where the cattle of Hyperion (the Sun) fed in verdant pastures. Circe had warned the voyagers that these flocks should be held inviolate, however pressing their wants might be. They were detained a long time at Thrinakia by contrary winds; and Ulys'ses bound his companions by an oath that they would not touch the sacred herds. They were, however, so pressed by famine that they ventured one day, in the absence of Ulys'ses, to slay a number of the sacred cattle; vainly endeavoring to propitiate the offended god, by offering a portion in sacrifice. Ulys'ses returning to the shore, was struck with horror at their temerity, the more so on account of the fearful signs which followed. The skins crept on the ground, and the joints of meat lowed on the spits while roasting.

As the wind was now favorable, Ulys'ses hastened to fly from the fatal island. The vengeance of the god pursued them on the sea, and a terrible storm arose, in which all perished, except Ulys'ses himself, who was spared as having taken no part in the sacrilege. He formed a raft from the fragments of his ship, and was at length cast by the waves upon the island of the nymph Calypso. This goddess entertained Ulys'ses with much kindness, and even offered to share her immortality with the hero, if he would consent to forget Ithaca and dwell forever in her happy island. Jupiter, however, sent Mercury to Calypso, with the command that she should dismiss Ulys'ses, and provide him with all that was necessary for his homeward voyage.

The goddess reluctantly obeyed; a raft was constructed and furnished, and Ulys'ses departed from the island. He sped prosperously for some days, and was almost within sight of land, when a violent storm arose, in which he would have perished had he not been aided by a compassion ate sea nymph; Minerva, also, smoothed the billows before him, and he swam safely to land.

The Phæacians, on whose shores he had been cast, received him kindly, and fitted out a ship in which he sailed for Ithaca. Ulys'ses was asleep when the vessel touched the strand. The Phæacians carried him on shore without awaking him, and placed near him a chest filled with costly gifts, after which they sailed away. Neptune was so much displeased with the Phæacians for aiding Ulys'ses, that, as their vessel was returning to port, he transformed it into a rock, which continued ever after to obstruct the mouth of their harbor.

The arrival of the hero could not have occurred more opportunely for the deliverance of his wife, the faithful Penel'ope. When a long time had elapsed after the fall of Troy, and no tidings were received of Ulys'ses, it was generally believed that he had perished. More than a hundred nobles of Ithaca and the surrounding islands, became suitors for the hand of Penel'ope; she however still cherished the hope of her husband's return, and refused to entertain any proposal of marriage. The suitors nevertheless persisted; they remained in the palace, which they filled with riot and feasting, and continually urged Penel'ope to choose a husband from among their number. She promised, at length, that she would do so when she had completed a certain web of embroidery on which she was engaged. They agreed to wait, and Penel'ope deceived them for a long time, plying her needle diligently during the day, and undoing the greater part of her work at night. This device succeeded for three years, at the end of which time the suitors became so importunate that Penel'ope could no longer resist. She promised, therefore, that she would marry that man who should send an arrow from the bow of Ulys'ses, through twelve rings suspended in a line. The conditions were accepted: and it was on the very eve of the day appointed for the contest, that Ulys'ses landed in Ithaca. It was necessary to conceal his return; for this purpose the hero disguised himself as a beggar, and by the aid of Minerva, so changed his whole appearance that it was impossible for any one to recognize him. In this character he was kindly received by Eumæus, a swine-herd, from whom he learned all that had transpired, and the present distress of Penel'ope.

Telem'achus, the son of Ulys'ses, had been absent for a long time in search of his father. He had visited the courts of the other kings who had taken part in the Trojan war, but without obtaining any certain tidings. While still engaged in this quest, Minerva bade him return to Ithaca; he obeyed, and the goddess contrived that he should arrive on the same day with his father, and meet him in the hut of Eumæus. After mutual explanations, and affectionate greetings, the two heroes consulted as to what measures they should take for the punishment of the suitors, and the deliverance of Penel'ope. It was resolved that Telem'achus should proceed to the palace, and mingle with the suitors, as formerly; that Ulys'ses should also go, but in the disguise of a beggar. Such persons were often admitted, in ancient times, to the halls of chieftains and princes, where they entertained the guests with stories of their wanderings, and were regaled with a portion of the viands. On their arrival at the palace, they found the usual scene of riot and festivity. The suitors received Telem'achus with affected joy, although secretly mortified at the failure of their plots against him. As Ulys'ses entered, a dog which lay in the court, half dead with age, raised his head in sudden recognition, fawned upon his old master, and expired. It was Argus, whom Ulys'ses had often led to the chase.

The banquet proceeded, but Telem'achus had much difficulty in dissembling his feelings when the suitors made his father a subject of mockery; and one of them carried his insolence so far as to strike the disguised hero. At length, the time arrived for the contest of skill which was to decide the fate of Penel'ope. Twelve rings were suspended at equal distances, and Telem'achus brought from the armory the mighty bow of Ulys'ses, with its quiver of arrows; taking care, at the same time, to remove all other weapons from the hall.

The first thing to be done, was to bend the bow, in order to attach the string. This Telem'achus tried to do, and was obliged to confess that his strength was unequal to the effort. He passed the bow to one of the suitors, who was compelled to yield it in turn, amid the raillery of his companions. When several had failed in the same manner, Ulys'ses begged that he might be allowed to try his skill. The request was received with shouts of derision, and some would have driven the insolent beggar from the hall. Telem'achus interfered, and remarking, with affected indifference, that they might as well gratify the old man, bade him try. Ulys'ses took the bow, and the suitors were amazed to see him handle the mighty weapon as if it had been a plaything. Their surprise was still greater, when, having adjusted the cord, and chosen an arrow from the quiver, he took such steady aim that the arrow sped unerringly through all the rings; he then exclaimed, "Now for another mark!" and aimed a second shaft at the most insolent of the suitors. He fell dead, and as the others rushed forward, Telem'achus placed himself by his father's side, with Eumæus and other armed retainers. The suitors, deprived of their weapons, and terrified at the aspect of the injured prince, whom they recognized too late, turned to fly, but Eumæus secured the doors. A desperate struggle ensued, in which all were slain, and Ulys'ses was left master of his palace and his kingdom. The Odyssey concludes with a description of the rejoicings which followed, and the happiness enjoyed by Ulys'ses and Penel'ope after their long separation. End.

CHAPTER XXXVI.

ORESTES.

Ques. Who was Orestes?

Ans. He was the son of Agamemnon and Clytemnestra. At the time of his father's assassination, Orestes, then a child, was saved by his sister Electra, who sent him secretly to their uncle Strophius, king of Phocis. Here he formed a friendship with Pylades, the son of that monarch, which was so true and constant that it passed into a proverb. Orestes was urged by messages from his sister Electra, to avenge the murder of his father, and her counsels were confirmed by the responses of the oracle of Apollo at Delphi. Orestes, accompanied by his friend Pyl'ades, repaired in disguise to Mycenæ. Here he announced himself to Clytemnestra as a messenger from Strophius, bringing news of the death of her son Orestes. The guilty queen feigned to grieve at these tidings, but Ægisthus made no effort to conceal his satisfaction. Orestes was now seized with horror at the thought of the deed which he was about to commit, but the reproaches of Elec tra, and the remembrance of his father's cruel fate, banished every thought of pity, and he slew Clytemnestra and Ægisthus with his own hand. This act, however justified by the guilt of Clytemnestra, and the express command of the gods, was abhorrent to nature, and could not pass unavenged. Orestes was pursued by the Furies, and wandered frantic and despairing from land to land, always accompanied by the faithful Pyl'ades.

The oracle of Apollo was consulted, and the Pythia declared that Orestes would not be delivered until he had visited the Tauric Chersone'sus, and brought from thence to Argos, a certain statue of Diana, from the temple of that goddess. It was the custom at Tauris, to sacrifice all strangers at the altar of Diana; Orestes and Pyl'ades were accordingly seized on their arrival, and carried as victims to the temple. The officiating priestess was no other than Iphigenia, the sister of Orestes, whom Diana had saved when she was about to be immolated at Aulis. Perceiving that the strangers were Greeks, she offered to spare the life of one, on condition that he would be the bearer of a letter to Greece.

This proposal gave rise to a memorable contest of friendship, each desiring to sacrifice himself for the other. Pyl'ades at length yielded to Orestes, and consented to take the letter. His surprise was great on perceiving that it was addressed to Orestes himself; an explanation followed, and Iphigenia resolved to fly from Tauris with her brother. Their plans were so well laid, that they not only succeeded in escaping unobserved, but were also enabled to carry off the statue of Diana, which they brought to Argos.

Orestes reigned many years in Mycenæ, and was married to his cousin Hermi'one, daughter of Menela'us and Helen. Pyl'ades married Electra, the sister of his friend.

The tragic poets add many incidents to the story of Orestes. They say that when pursued by the Furies, he took refuge in the temple of Apollo, at Delphi. By the command of that god, he repaired to Athens, where he was tried by the court of Areop'agus. The judges were divided in their sentiments, but Minerva interfered in behalf of Orestes, and he was acquitted.

HECTOR.

Ques. Who was Hector?

Ans. He was the son of Priam and Hec'uba, and the most valiant of all the Trojan chiefs who fought against the Greeks. The Fates had decreed that Troy should not be taken as long as Hector lived. The hero knew that he was destined to fall before the walls of his native city, and that he could at best only postpone the ruin of his country for a little time. Not discouraged by this, he performed prodigies of valor, and slew, with his own hand, Patroclus, the friend of Achil'les. He next went out to meet Achil'les himself notwithstanding the remonstrances of Priam and Hec'uba, and the tears of his wife Androm'ache. He, fell as we have seen, and this event was shortly followed by the overthrow of his father's kingdom. Hector was not only distinguished as a warrior and a patriot; he was equally admirable as a son, husband, and father; and his character is perhaps the noblest which has been described by any writer of antiquity.

When Troy was taken, Calchas excited much uneasiness among the Greeks, by a prediction, that if Asty'anax, the son of Hector, were permitted to live, he would one day avenge his father's death, and raise Troy from its ruins. Diligent search was therefore made for the child, who had been concealed by his mother in the recesses of Hector's tomb. Here he was discovered by Ulys'ses. Disregarding the prayers of the unhappy Androm'ache, the Grecian commanders precipitated the boy from the summit of a lofty tower

ŒDIPUS—ETEOCLES AND POLYNICES.

Ques. What was the story of these princes?

Ans. Œdipus was the son of La'ius, king of Thebes. He was exposed by his father immediately on his birth, to avoid the fulfillment of an oracle which declared that La'ius was destined to fall by the hand of one of his children. Œdipus was found by a herdsman, who brought him to

Pol'ybus, king of Corinth. This monarch was childless, and adopted the infant as his own.

When Œdipus was grown to manhood, he desired to learn something of his real parentage, and went to consult the oracle of Delphi. The god warned him to shun his native country, declaring that if he returned thither, he would become the murderer of his father, and be guilty of crimes which would draw upon him the vengeance of the gods. Œdipus understood this of Corinth, and instead of returning to that city, proceeded to Thebes Here he slew his father La'ius in an accidental encounter, and, after his victory over the Sphinx, which we have already mentioned, he fulfilled the other predictions of the oracle.

Œdipus reigned many years in Thebes before he discovered his parentage, and the crimes which he had unknowingly committed. In his despair, he put out his eyes, and went into exile, leaving the throne to his sons Ete'ocles and Polyni'ces. It was agreed between the brothers that they should reign each a year alternately. Ete'ocles first ascended the throne; but when the year had expired, he refused to resign the crown. Polyni'ces was indignant at this breach of faith, and fled to Argos, where he married the daughter of King Adrastus. This monarch assembled a large army to enforce the claims of his son-in-law. The command of the expedition was given to seven chieftains, who were to attack each one of the seven gates of Thebes.

After all the Argive leaders, except Adrastus, had perished before the walls, it was proposed that Ete'ocles and Polyni'ces should decide the war by single combat. The brothers fought with such animosity that both fell, mortally wounded. The battle was then renewed, and the Argives were totally defeated. Creon, the uncle of the fallen princes, was now king of Thebes; he had the body of Ete'ocles honorably buried, but he left the remains of Polyni'ces exposed to the dogs and vultures, and forbade, under pain of death, that any one should bestow on him the rites of sepulture. He thus carried his vengeance beyond the grave, as, according to Greek superstition, the souls of the unburied were excluded for a hundred years from the Elysian fields.

Antig'one, the daughter of Œdipus, had, meanwhile, accompanied her father in his exile, and watched over him with touching devotion until death released her from this filial duty. She no sooner learned the cruel order of Creon, than she resolved, at whatever hazard, to perform the funeral rites for Polyni'ces. She succeeded in approaching the corpse, which she covered with earth, making the usual libations.

While thus engaged, Antig'one was seized and brought before Creon. She defended nobly the pious act which she had performed, and was condemned by the tyrant to be entombed alive.

The misfortunes of Œdipus and his children have been celebrated by three Greek tragedians Æschylus, Sophocles and Euripides. In the tragedy of Sophocles which bears her name, the character of Antig'one is beautifully drawn. We have the sternest heroism, tempered always by the tenderness of filial piety and sisterly devotion. The whole presents the finest ideal of womanly excellence which can be found in the writings of any ancient poet.

The following lines are taken from Dale's translation of the Antig'one. Creon reproaches the heroine with having violated the laws; she replies:

'Ne'er did eternal Jove such laws ordain,
Or Justice, throned amid th' infernal powers,
Who on mankind these holier rites imposed—
Nor can I deem thine edict armed with power
To contravene the firm unwritten laws
Of the just gods, thyself a weak frail mortal!
. . . . I knew before
That I must die, though thou had'st ne'er proclaimed it,
And if I perish ere th' allotted term,
I deem that death a blessing. Who that lives
Like me encompassed by unnumbered ills,
But would account it blessedness to die?
If then I meet the doom thy laws assign,
It nothing grieves me. Had I left my brother,
From my own mother sprung, on the bare earth
To lie unburied, that, indeed, might grieve me;
But for this deed I mourn not." . . .

CHAPTER XXXVII.

ÆNEAS.

Ques. Who was Æne'as?

Ans. He was a Trojan chief, the son of Venus and Anchi'ses. He was born on Mount Ida, where he was nurtured by the Dryads until he had attained his fifth year, when he was brought to his father. Anchi'ses was not on friendly terms with the family of Priam, but this coldness did not prevent Æne'as from exerting himself to the utmost in defence of his country. Excepting Hector only, there was no Trojan who so distinguished himself by his valor. When Troy was taken, Æne'as made his escape from the burning city, bearing on his shoulders the aged Anchi'ses, and leading his little son Ascanius by the hand. His wife was separated from him in the confusion and darkness, and perished by the sword of the enemy. Anchises bore with him the sacred Penates of Troy, and his household gods. Æne'as was joined by the greater part of the Trojans, both men and women, who had escaped from the horrors of that fatal night. They concealed themselves in the neighboring mountains until the Greeks had departed, after which they constructed a fleet of twenty sail. In the second year after the destruction of Troy, the remnant of the Trojans embarked under the guidance of Æne'as in search of new settlements. After many wanderings and adventures, they landed at Epi'rus, and were rejoiced to learn that Hel'enus, one of the sons of Priam, was reigning in that country. He had married Androm'ache, and the meeting of Æne'as with the widow of the great Hector is the subject of a very beautiful passage in the Æneid. The Penates of Troy had appeared at night to Anchi'ses, and revealed to him that Italy was the land allotted by the Fates to the exiled Trojans. Æne'as recalled a prediction of Cassandra to the same effect; and Hel'enus, who was endowed with the gift of prophecy, now confirmed what had been already foretold. He rendered his exiled countrymen all the assistance in his power, and dismissed them at length, loaded with costly gifts. Æne'as was destined to pass through many perils before landing on the shores of Italy. In the seventh year of their wanderings, the Trojans were driven by a storm on the coast of Africa; here they were kindly entertained by Dido, who was then engaged in the erection of her new city of Carthage. The queen admired the great qualities of the Trojan chief, and felt her heart moved with compassion at the sight of so much undeserved misfortune. She resolved, therefore, to share her throne with the hero, and to offer his followers a permanent settlement in the country. This proposal seems not to have been displeasing either to Æne'as or to the Trojans. Forgetful of the decrees of fate, they lingered many months in idle pleasure, and Æne'as was only roused to action by the direct intervention of the gods. Jupiter sent Mercury to the hero, commanding him to embark without delay, and proceed to his destined settlement in Italy. Æne'as obeyed, and made the necessary preparations for departure, disregarding the tears and reproaches of the queen.

When Dido found that all was unavailing, and that the Trojans had already embarked, she killed herself in despair.

Æne'as spent some time in Sicily, where he celebrated funeral games in honor of his father, who had died there the preceding year. He left with Acestes, a Trojan prince who governed a part of the island, the women, the aged men, and all who were likely to be useless in the wars which awaited him. Æne'as next landed at Cumæ, in Italy. This was the abode of a famous Sibyl, of whom we will speak elsewhere. She foretold to the hero much that was to happen during his settlement in Italy; but in order that he might be fully informed of the future destinies of his race, she offered to conduct him to the world of shades. Æne'as having plucked, in the sacred grove, a golden bough as a gift to Proser'pine, descended

with the Sibyl to the dreary realms of Pluto
After seeing much that was wonderful, and passing through regions inhabited by different classes of departed souls, they entered the happy plains of Elysium. This was the abode of the heroes and other favorites of the gods. Here, in a fragrant meadow, Æne'as found the shade of Anchi'ses, who showed him the souls which were destined to return to earth, and become the future heroes of Rome. Anchi'ses also recounted to Æne'as the glorious deeds which they were one day to perform. In this passage, Virgil takes occasion to gratify the vanity of Augustus and the great families of Rome, by introducing their names and actions in the prophetic discourse of Anchi'ses.

Returning to upper air, Æne'as took leave of the sibyl, and pursued his voyage along the Italian coast, anchoring at length in the mouth of the Tiber.

The country around was governed by a prince named Latinus, the son of Faunus and the nymph Marica. This prince had one child, a daughter named Lavinia. Her hand had been promised to Turnus, prince of the Rutulians, but Latinus was warned by an oracle that his destined son-in-law was to come from afar, and that Lavinia was to wed a foreigner. When Æne'as sent an embassy to Latinus, requesting permission to settle in the country, that prince believed that the Trojan chief was the person pointed out by the oracle, and invited him to his palace. All now seemed to promise a peaceful settlement to the harassed Trojans, but the enmity of Juno was not yet appeased. She sent the Fury Alecto to the palace of Turnus, with orders to excite this prince against the stranger, who was about to rob him of his promised bride. A long war ensued, which forms the subject of the concluding books of the Æneid. At length Turnus fell in a personal combat with Æne'as. The hand of Lavinia was the price of victory, and from the Trojan hero were descended the founders of Rome.

The Æneid concludes with the death of Turnus, but we have some further particulars handed down by tradition. Æneas built a city, called from his bride, Lavinium. Here he governed his Trojan and Italian subjects, who became one people under the common name of Latins. The new kingdom was attacked by several of the neighboring princes, led by Mezentius, king of Etruria. Æneas defeated the allies, but was killed in the moment of victory. The family of Julii, made illustrious by Julius Cæsar, claimed descent from Iulus, grandson of Æneas.

CHAPTER XXXVIII.

SIBYLS—AUGURS

Ques. Who were the Sibyls?

Ans. The Sibyllæ, or Sibyls, were certain females, supposed to be inspired by Heaven, who flourished at different times and in different parts of the world. According to the historian Varro, they were ten in number. The most celebrated was the Cumæan Sibyl, of whom the poets give the following account. Apollo sought the love of the young prophetess, and promised to give her whatever she should demand. The sibyl desired that she might live as many years as she had grains of sand in her hand; but as she forgot to ask for health and youthful bloom, this long life proved rather a burden than a benefit. She had rejected the suit of Apollo, and the god refused, therefore, to withdraw his gift or mitigate the severity of her lot. This sibyl had already lived seven hundred years when Æne'as came to Italy, and six centuries still remained of the time granted by Apollo. She accompanied Æne'as on his visit to the lower world. According to a well-known Roman legend, one of the sibyls came to the palace of the second Tarquin with nine volumes, which she offered to sell at a very high price. The king declined the offer; the sibyl immediately disappeared and burned three of the volumes. Returning soon after, she asked the same price for the remaining six books; and when Tarquin again refused to buy them, she burned three more, and still persisted in demanding the same sum of money for those that were left. This extraordinary conduct astonished the monarch, and with the advice of the Augurs he bought the books, upon which the sibyl disappeared and was never seen after. These books were preserved with great care, and were called the Sibylline Verses. A college of priests was appointed to take charge of them, and·they were consulted with the greatest solemnity, whenever the state seemed to be in danger. When the Capitol was burned in the troubles raised by Sylla, the Sibylline Verses are said by some to have perished in the conflagration. It is believed, however, on good authority, that they were in existence as late as the fourth century, when they were destroyed by command of the Emperor Honorius. Various collections were afterwards made, which are generally admitted to be forgeries.

Different opinions have prevailed with regard to the prophecies of the sibyls, some of which, it is said, pointed clearly to the advent of a Redeemer, the time of his coming, and the submission of Rome to the new dispensation. It has been thought that these passages were invented by later Christian writers, but Bishop Horsley, a learned English divine, thinks it more reasonable to suppose that the sibylline books contained the records of prophecies which were granted in primitive times, to nations outside of the patriarchal and Jewish races. He cites in favor of this opinion, the fact that St. Justin, in his apology addressed to the Emperor Marcus Antoninus, appeals confidently to the sibylline prophecies, and at that time, about the middle of the second century, it was not possible that the Christians should have added anything to them. There are also passages in the fourth Eclogue of Virgil which prove that the expectation of a Saviour, and the belief that the time of his advent was approaching, existed even among the pagans.

Divination by Omens—The Augurs.

Ques. Who were the Augurs?

Ans. They were priests whose office it was to observe and interpret omens. This science was derived from the ancient Etrurians. There were five principal classes of omens from which the Augurs were supposed to foretell future events, the good or ill success of an undertaking, etc. The first were drawn from the phenomena of nature, such as thunder, lightning, comets, etc. The second kind of omen was obtained by observing the cries and the flight of birds. In the third class we may place the appetite of the sacred chickens; when they did not eat, the omen was so bad that it was considered unlucky to give battle, or undertake anything of importance. It happened once that a Roman commander, (Claudius Pulcher,) when about to engage the fleet of the enemy, was warned by the Augurs that the sacred chickens would not eat. He replied, with very natural contempt, that if they would not eat, they might drink, and had them thrown into the sea. It is believed that the terrible defeat the Romans suffered on that day was owing, in great part, to the discouragement of the sailors, who supposed that their commander had forfeited the favor of the gods by this act of sacrilege.

Omens were drawn from the appearance of the entrails of animals offered in sacrifice, also from the meeting with quadrupeds in any unaccustomed place.

The fifth class of omens was taken from different casualties, such as spilling salt, stumbling on the threshold, sneezing, meeting a hare, wolf, fox, etc. Some of these last superstitions prevail, more or less, to the present day.

CHAPTER XXXIX.

ORACLES.

Ques. What do you understand by oracles?

Ans. The places where the heathen divinities were supposed to answer those who consulted them, were called oracles. This word was also applied to the responses given.

Ques. Name some of the more famous oracles?

Ans. Among the most celebrated were, the oracles of Jupiter at Dodo'na; of Apollo, at Delphi; of Trophonius, near Lebe'dea in Bœotia; of Jupiter Ammon, in the deserts of Lybia; of Æsculapius at Epidaurus; and the Castalian Fount.

Ques. Describe the oracle of Dodo'na.

Ans. Dodo'na was a town of Epirus, probably situated in the valley now called Joannina, but the exact site has not been ascertained. In the earlier times Jupiter gave answers to his votaries by means of a so-called vocal oak or beach. Brazen instruments, suspended from the higher branches, clashed together when moved by the wind. The priestesses who were appointed to explain the responses of the oracle could attach whatever meaning they pleased to these inarticulate sounds. Later, the Corcyrians presented to the temple a brazen caldron surmounted by a figure of the same metal; the statue held in its hand a whip, the lash of which consisted of three chains, each having an astragalus (a small bone) at the end. These, when moved by the winds, struck the caldron, and produced so continuous a sound that four hundred vibrations were sometimes counted before it ceased. Demosthenes tells us that the responses delivered to the Athenians at Dodo'na were carefully preserved in the public archives; their reverence for the oracle did not, however, prevent them from accusing the priestess of being influenced by bribes when they were dissatisfied with her answers.

The oracle of Dodo'na was probably the most ancient in Greece. The temple was founded by the Pelasgi long before the siege of Troy; it was partially destroyed by the Ætolians during the Social War, and it would seem that it never recovered from this disaster. The town existed many centuries later; and we read of a bishop of Dodo'na who attended the council of Ephesus.

Ques. What does Diodorus tell us concerning the oracle at Delphi?

Ans. This historian relates that a shepherd, while feeding his flocks on the side of Mount Parnassus, observed that his sheep and goats, on approaching a certain cavity in the earth, began to skip and dance about in an extraordinary manner. As he drew near to examine the cause of this phenomenon, the vapors, exhaling from the earth, affected him in the same way; his body was convulsed, and he spoke words which revealed futurity. Others experienced similar effects, and the exhalation was supposed to have a certain divine property. The cavity was approached with reverence; a tripod was placed over it; and a priestess or Pythia was appointed to preside. The words which she uttered when under the influence of the vapor were considered to be inspired by Apollo; crowds came to consult the oracle; a temple was built, and the city of Delphi arose insensibly around the spot.

As the oracle grew in repute it became necessary to appoint a second and a third Pythia to answer those who came to consult the god. The Pythia could not prophesy until she had become intoxicated by the vapor from the sanctuary. This effect was not produced at all times, and on some days it was not permitted to consult the oracle. Spring was considered the most propitious season. When Apollo was favorably disposed, his approach was made known by the moving of a laurel that stood before the gate of the temple. The sacred tree was then seen to tremble in every leaf.

The Pythia was obliged to prepare by fasts, sacrifices and purifications before she ascended the tripod. When under the influence of the mysterious vapor, her hair stood erect, her eyes flashed, she foamed at the mouth, and a convulsive trembling seized her whole body.

She then spoke prophetic words, which were carefully noted by the attendant priests. The oracles were sometimes in verse, but more commonly in prose; in the latter case they were immediately versified by poets employed for that purpose.

Many remarkable oracles are recorded by Herodotus as having been delivered at Delphi, but as a general thing the answers were ambiguous, and so cautiously worded as to seem true, whatever might be the event. Such was the answer given to Crœ'sus, king of Lydia, when he consulted the oracle concerning the result of his expedition against the Medes. The Pythia told him that by crossing the river Halys he would ruin a great empire, but as she did not say what empire, whether his own or that of his enemies, the oracle could not fail of being fulfilled. There is no doubt that the Pythia was often influenced by persuasion or bribes, and many illustrious persons were accused of having bought the oracles they desired.

The temple of Apollo at Delphi was enriched by the offerings of different princes, and the surrounding nations vied with one another in the magnificence of their gifts. The building was destroyed by fire in the year 548 B. C., but was soon rebuilt. Xerxes, after having forced the pass of Thermopylæ, sent a detachment of his army to plunder the treasures of Delphi. The expedition was unsuccessful, owing, as the Delphians asserted, to a manifest interposition of the deity. Afterwards, Philome'lus, a Phocian general, seized these treasures to pay his troops. He is said to have carried off, in gold and silver, a sum equal to ten million dollars. Still later Delphi was threatened by the Gauls, under their king Brennus. According to Pausanias, the city and temple were saved by Pan, as we have seen in the account given of that god; but others declare that the invaders possessed themselves of great booty. Sylla also plundered Delphi, and Nero took from it, at one time, no less than five hundred statues of bronze.

The temple was finally dismantled by Constantine the Great, who adorned his Hippodrome with the sacred tripods

No traces are known to exist of the cavern whence issued the sacred vapor, but some have thought it might be discovered by searching in the central part of the ruins of the ancient city.

Ques. Who was Trophonius, and for what was his oracle remarkable?

Ans. Trophonius, and his brother Agame'des were the architects of the temple of Apollo at Delphi. According to one legend, when the edifice was finished, they asked the god to reward them for their labor. Apollo promised that he would recompense them on the seventh day, and bade them live happily during the interval. On the seventh night the brothers died in their sleep. The oracle is said to have been discovered on the following occasion: In a time of severe drought the Bœotians consulted Apollo at Delphi, and were directed to seek aid from Trophonius in Lebadea. They proceeded thither, and seeing a swarm of bees enter a chasm in the earth, they followed and discovered a deep cavern. Here they found the oracle of Trophonius, and the aid they sought.

Ques. What ceremonies were observed in consulting this oracle?

Ans. The votary was first purified by solemn ablutions; then, after offering sacrifice, and drinking of a water called Lethe, or oblivion, he descended by means of ladders into the first, or upper cavern. The opening into the lower cave was extremely narrow, and there was apparently nothing to aid the descent. Here, those who were courageous enough to advance, lay upon the ground with their feet within the entrance, taking care to hold in each hand a certain composition of honey. They were then carried downwards with great force, as by the current of a rapid river. In the mysterious depths of the lower cave, the future was revealed, but not to all in the same manner; some saw, others heard what they desired to know.

It has been frequently asserted that those who entered the cave of Trophonius never smiled and we should judge, from the accounts given by ancient writers, that they were subjected to a treatment closely resembling what we now call animal magnetism, or mesmerism.

Ques. Where was the temple of **Jupiter Ammon**?

Ans. It was situated in an oasis of the Libyan desert, called by the ancients Ammon, and by the modern Arabs, Siwah. It is about five degrees west of Cairo.

The temple is said to have been founded by Bacchus under the following circumstances. While marching through the Libyan desert, Bacchus came to a barren waste of sand where his whole army was in danger of perishing for want of water. He called on Jupiter for aid, and a ram suddenly appeared, which guided them to a verdant oasis, in the midst of which sparkled a clear fountain. Bacchus erected on the spot, a temple which he dedicated to Jupiter. As the surrounding country was called Hammo'des from Hammon or Ammon, sand, the god was worshipped here under this title, and was always represented as having the head and horns of a ram. The temple soon became celebrated as an oracle, and was enriched, like that of Delphi, by splendid offerings. When Camby'ses invaded Egypt, he sent a large body of troops across the desert to seize its treasures. As nothing was ever heard of this expedition, it seems probable that the Persians were purposely misled by their Egyptian guides, and thus perished in the desert. Alexander the Great visited the temple of Jupiter Ammon to question the oracle as to his parentage; and the priests, who were undoubtedly apprised of the object of his visit, did not wait to be questioned, but saluted the king as the son of Jupiter. The site of this temple was discovered in the last century by an English traveller, but the latest and best account is given by Belzoni, who visited it in 1816. The oasis is about six miles in length, with an average breadth of four miles. It is fertile and produces in abundance, rice, wheat and fruits. The ruins of the temple are not extensive; they are, however, interesting, as many pieces of sculpture, including figures of goats with rams' heads, are found in a good state of preservation. In a beautiful grove of palms, towards the centre of the oasis, is the famous Fons Solis, or Fountain of the Sun, which does not, however, correspond with the description given by Herodotus. According to that historian, this fountain was always tepid at dawn, icy cold at noon; it grew warm again towards sunset, and was boiling hot at midnight. Belzoni says that this account is quite exaggerated, although the water of the fountain felt to him much warmer at midnight than at noon-day. The truth seems to be that little or no change takes place in the fountain, which is well shaded and very deep. The great change which really takes place in the atmosphere is probably the cause of the apparent variation in the temperature of the fountain. Belzoni had no thermometer with him, so that he was unable to test the truth of this supposition.

Ques. Where was the oracle of Æsculapius?

Ans. This god was consulted by the sick in many places, but his most celebrated oracle was in his native city of Epidaurus in Argolis. This oracle was so famous that in the year 293 B. C., when a terrible pestilence was raging in Rome, the Senate sent a solemn embassy to Epidaurus to implore the aid of Æsculapius. The god was propitious, and accompanied the returning embassy in the form of a serpent. According to another account, the priests sent to Rome a sacred serpent which they nourished in the temple.

Ques. What was particularly remarkable in the oracles of Æsculapius?

Ans. It would seem that the priests, who had probably some skill in medicine, made use of every means calculated to encourage the votaries, and inspire them with a confident hope of recovery. They were obliged to sleep in the temple, and we should judge, from the accounts given by ancient writers, that they were subjected to a treatment closely resembling what we now call animal magnetism, or mesmerism.

The temple of Epidaurus was plundered by Sylla to defray the expenses of the war against Mithridates.

Ques. Where was the Castalian Fount?

Ans. There were two celebrated springs of that

name; one on Mount Parnassus, which was sacred to the Muses, and another near Daphne, in Syria. This last was believed to impart the knowledge of futurity to those who drank of its waters. The oracle of this fountain promised the empire to Hadrian, while he was yet in a private station. When he ascended the throne, he had the fountain shut up with stones.

Ques. What opinions did the early Christian writers hold with regard to the heathen oracles?

Ans. They believed that although the responses were to be attributed, as a general thing, to mere human jugglery and imposture, there were occasions in which it was impossible to doubt the direct agency of evil spirits. We read in Scripture that Satan spoke by the mouths of the possessed, and none were more likely to fall under this demoniac influence than the priests and other ministrants in these shrines of imposture. Many instances are recorded where Christians imposed silence on oracles by pronouncing the name of Jesus Christ, or by the sign of the cross; and sometimes the same effect was produced by their simple presence in the temple.

Ques. At what period did the oracles cease to give responses?

Ans. No exact date can be assigned; as Christianity spread, these impostures fell gradually into disrepute, and were at length entirely abandoned. It has been asserted that the oracles became silent at the birth of Christ, but this is an error. Milton, however adopts this idea in his beautiful Hymn of the Nativity

"The oracles are dumb;
　No voice or hideous hum
　　Rings through the arched roof in words deceiving.
Apollo from his shrine
Can no more divine,
　　With hollow shriek the steep of Delphos leaving.
No nightly trance or breathed spell
　Inspires the pale-eyed priest from the prophetic cell.'

CHAPTER XL.

CLASSIC GAMES.

Ques. Why is a notice of these games appropriate in this place?

Ans. Because they were closely connected with the religious observances of the Greeks. They were begun and ended with solemn sacrifices, and formed a part in the celebration of the principal festivals held in honor of the gods. These remarks apply also to the Greek drama.

Ques. What games were solemnized in Greece?

Ans. They were of four kinds: the Olympic, the Pythian, the Ne'mean, and the Isthmian.

Ques. Who instituted the Olympic games?

Ans. They were very ancient; their first institution was attributed by the Greeks to Hercules. They were revived by Iphitus, king of Elis, who obtained for them the solemn sanction of the Delphic oracle. The Olympian games were celebrated at intervals of forty-nine and fifty lunar months alternately, so that they fell sometimes in the month Apollonius, (July); sometimes in the month Parthenius, (August). The time of their celebration was a period of sacred truce, sufficiently prolonged to enable persons to attend the games from every part of Greece, and return to their homes in safety. The interval between the celebrations was called an Olympiad, and the Greeks usually counted time in this manner. The Olympiads were reckoned only from the year 776, B. C., although the games had been revived by Iphitus more than a century earlier. The Olympic festival lasted five days. The games consisted of chariot, horse and foot races; leaping, wrestling, boxing, throwing the discus or quoit, etc. All persons were admitted to contend in these games who could prove that they were free, of pure Hellenic blood, and that their characters had never been stained by any base or immoral act. So great was the importance attached to race, that even the kings of Macedon were obliged to prove their Hellenic descent before they were allowed to enter as competitors. It is almost impossible for us to realize the importance attached by the Greeks to a victory gained in any of these exercises. The prize itself was a crown of wild olive. This was cut from a tree in the sacred grove of Olympia, which was said to have been brought by Hercules from the land of the Hyperboreans. A palm branch was at the same time placed in the victor's hand, and his name was proclaimed by the herald. On his return home, more distinguished honors awaited him. He entered his native city, not by the gate, but through a breach made in the walls for his reception. Banquets were given to him by his friends, at which odes were sung in honor of his victory. The horse and chariot races held the highest rank, and singularly enough, the honor of the victory belonged to the owner of the horse or chariot, although he himself should not have been present at the games.

The Greek historians relate that three couriers were received by Philip of Macedon on the same day, each being the bearer of joyful tidings. The first announced that his general had gained a great victory; the second, that his horse had won the prize in the Olympic games; while the third brought news of the birth of his son, afterwards Alexander the Great. This passage is sufficient to show what importance was attached to such a victory, when we see it thus classed as an event of equal importance with the success of an army, and the birth of an heir to a great kingdom.

Alcibiades on one occasion entered seven four-horse chariots in the Olympic games, and carried off the first, second and third prizes. The poet Euripides celebrated this victory, and Alcibiades, after offering solemn sacrifices to Jupiter, feasted the entire multitude assembled to witness the games. Ladies were admitted to dispute the prizes at Olympia, and many are mentioned as successful competitors. Cynisca, the sister of Agesilaus, king of Sparta, first opened this path of glory to her sex, and was proclaimed conqueror in the four-horse chariot race. This victory, till then unexampled, was celebrated with all possible splendor. A magnificent monument was erected in Sparta in honor of Cynisca, and the Lacedæmonians, who were generally indifferent to the charms of verse, engaged a poet to transmit this new triumph to posterity. The princess dedicated a brazen chariot in the temple of Apollo at Delphi; in this votive offering, the charioteer was also represented; which proves that she had not driven the chariot herself at the games. This is a feat which, it is believed, no woman ever attempted. The portrait of Cynisca, drawn by the great Apelles, was afterwards placed in the same temple.

Ques. Were any other exercises admitted at the Olympic games?

Ans. Yes; there was also an intellectual competition, which was perhaps more lively and ardent than any other, as the victory in such a contest was more highly esteemed. The best writers and poets of Greece repaired to the Olympic games, believing that the approbation of so illustrious an assembly was the most certain means of establishing a great reputation in a little time. It was thus that Herodotus read his history to assembled Greece. It was received with enthusiastic applause, and the names of the nine muses were immediately given to the nine books which compose the work. Dionysius was not so fortunate. This prince believed himself the most excellent poet of the time, and employed professional readers to recite some of his pieces at Olympia. When they began to read these verses their clear and harmonious voices pleased the ear, and they were listened to at first with great attention, which gradually decreased as they went on, until the whole assembly burst forth into hooting and shouts of laughter, so absurd did the pretensions of the royal poet appear.

What we have said of the Olympic Games, may be applied with some little variation to those solemnized in other places.

Ques. By whom were the Pythian Games instituted?

Ans. According to Greek fable, by Apollo himself, in commemoration of his victory over the serpent Python; according to the more probable historic account, they originated at the time when the Delphic oracle had already gained some reputation. The Amphictyonic council was charged with the superintendence of the games, which were celebrated at first every ninth, and afterwards every fifth year. The crown bestowed was of bay.

Ques. Where were the Ne'mean games celebrated?

Ans. At Ne'mea, a city of Argolis, celebrated as the haunt of the lion slain by Hercules. They were said to have been restored by that hero, and were celebrated every third year. The crowns bestowed on the victors were of parsley, because these were originally funeral games, and it was customary to lay chaplets of parsley on the tombs of the dead. The ruins of Ne'mea are to be seen near the modern village of Kutchumadi.

Ques. Why were the Isthmian Games so called?

Ans. They were named from the Isthmus of Corinth, where they were celebrated. They were instituted in honor of Melicertes, who was changed into a sea deity. After falling into neglect, these games were restored by Theseus. They were celebrated every five years, and continued to be solemnized even after the destruction of Corinth by the Romans. The victors were at first rewarded with garlands of pine leaves, but this custom was changed, and the pine was replaced by a crown of withered **parsley**.

CHAPTER XLI.

THEATRES.

Ques. Did the theatrical representations of the Greeks resemble those of modern times?

Ans. They differed widely, both in the arrangement of the drama, and the mode of representation. The greatest distinction lay, perhaps, in the structure of the theatre itself.

Ques. Describe the general plan of a Greek theatre?

Ans. It was quite open above, and the dramas were always acted in the light of day, beneath the bright canopy of a southern heaven. The Romans at a later period introduced awnings to screen the audience from the sun, but the Greeks would have regarded such a precaution as a mark of effeminacy; and it must be admitted that their milder climate rendered it almost unnecessary. If a storm or a shower came on, the play was, of course, interrupted; the gods and heroes disappeared, and the audience sought shelter in the lofty colonnade which always ran behind their seats. They chose to suffer these occasional in-

conveniences, rather than shut themselves up in
a close and crowded house, and forfeit the sunny
brightness of what was to them a national, and
even, in some sort, religious solemnity. To have
covered in the stage itself, and imprisoned gods
and heroes in a gloomy apartment artificially
lighted, would have appeared to the ancients in
the highest degree absurd.

The great theatre of Bacchus, at Athens, is the
only structure of the kind of which a complete
description has reached us. It may serve to give
a general idea of these edifices.

This theatre stood on the southeastern side of
the eminence which was crowned by the noble
buildings of the Acropolis. From the level of the
plain below, a semicircular excavation ascended
far up on the slope of the hill. Round the con-
cavity, seats for an audience of thirty thousand
persons arose, range above range; higher still,
the whole was enclosed by a lofty portico adorned
with statues and surmounted by a balustraded
terrace. For the convenience of entering and
leaving, the tiers of benches were divided at intervals, by passages extending around the theatre,
and again transversely, into wedge-like masses,
by flights of steps which radiated from the lowest
tier to the portico above. The lower seats, being
more conveniently placed for seeing and hearing,
were esteemed the most honorable, and were reserved for the high magistrates, the priests and
the Senate. Below, was the semicircular orches-

tra, or pit, which was generally occupied by the chorus. Elevated above the orchestra, and opposite the lower seats, was the stage itself. This had a very wide front and but little depth. The actors usually spoke in the central part, called logeum, or pulpitum. Behind this, the stage grew deeper, and formed a quadrangle called the proscenium. This was enclosed by lofty buildings of stone-work, representing externally a palace-like mansion, and containing within withdrawing rooms for the actors, and receptacles for the stage machinery. When the nature of the play rendered it necessary, these buildings were concealed by painted scenes. In the greater number of tragedies, however, the whole action might be carried on appropriately enough in the portico or court of a palace. There were also contrivances by which a portion of the interior might be exposed to view. The rank of the personages was generally indicated by the particular door at which they entered; that in the centre of the proscenium being reserved for royalty. Wonderful effects were produced by the use of the machinery which was disposed behind the walls of the stage. Supported by ropes, or iron cranes, carefully concealed, gods appeared in the air, descended on the stage, and performed their allotted part in the drama. Heroes also ascended to Olympus, and were hidden at length from view by scenic clouds. In the Prometheus of Æschylus, Oceanus passes through the air, mounted on a griffin, and a choir of fifteen ocean nymphs is introduced in a flying chariot. In another piece, Aurora descends and carries off the dead body of Memnon. Ghosts and infernal deities ascended from beneath the stage, where there were appropriate contrivances for their introduction. When it was necessary to conceal the stage, the curtain was not dropped, but drawn up from beneath the floor.

Ques. Was there anything peculiar in the dress of the actors?

Ans. The costumes were splendid, and carefully adapted to the rank and character of the personages represented. The actors wore masks which covered the entire head. When gods or heroic personages were represented, the masks were larger than life, and the disproportion of the size of the head with the rest of the body, was obviated by two different contrivances. The cothurnus, or buskin, was soled with several layers of cork, which added at least three inches to the height of the actor, and the dress was judiciously padded, so as to give the whole figure the necessary heroic dimensions. Women were not admitted on the Greek stage; the female parts were always performed by men, wearing appropriate wigs and masks.

It has been supposed that the use of masks must have embarrassed the actors, and made them appear stiff and unnatural. This may have been true to a certain extent, but we must remember that, at the distance at which the actors were placed from the greater part of their audience, the changes of expression, and the play of feature would have been quite lost, while the large and finely colored masks may have had a very good effect. Nothing would have seemed more out of place to the Greeks, than to see the part of Apollo or Hercules performed by an actor with strongly marked or ordinary features.

The masks were lined with brass, and so constructed that instead of muffling the voice, they gave it depth and volume, almost as a speaking trumpet would have done.

Ques. What was the Chorus?

Ans. It was a choir of singers, varying in number from fifteen to fifty. In the intervals between the acts of the drama, the chorus chanted verses corresponding to the action of the piece, sometimes pouring forth hymns of thanksgiving or supplication to the gods; sometimes chanting odes on the instability of human affairs as exemplified in the scenes which they had just witnessed. At other times the chorus broke forth into lamentations over the untimely fate of some personage of the drama, or denounced the anger of the gods on the head of a tyrant. Besides this more legitimate action of the chorus, it was occasionally permitted to take part in the dialogue. Even in this case they always remained in the orchestra.

The singing was always accompanied by dances which varied according to the nature of the piece.

All the movements of a tragic chorus were slow and grave, while in the lighter pieces, the music and the measures of the dance were quick and lively. The dress of the chorus varied in the same manner. In certain tragedies, these singers personated the Eumenides or Furies. These were generally robed in black, with purple girdles. They brandished whips, wreathed with serpents, in their fleshless hands, and their aspect was rendered still more terrible by the frightful masks which appeared beneath their snaky tresses. We are told that when Æschylus introduced such a chorus in one of his tragedies, the terror of the spectators was such that many fainted, and several children died of fright.

In this connection we have an interesting story. Ibycus, a lyric poet, was on his way to the Isthmian games, when he was waylaid by two robbers. The unhappy bard called in vain for aid; no human help was near; but his last, despairing cry was echoed by the hoarse scream of a flock of cranes which was passing overhead. The dying poet heard, and looking upwards, prayed the birds to discover and avenge the crime which they alone had seen. The murderers heard this appeal, to which, however, they paid no heed at the time. The body of Ibycus was found and recognized, and the multitude assembled to witness the Isthmian games were sorely disappointed and dismayed at the sad tidings of his death. They crowded the tribunals and demanded vengeance on the murderers, but no trace could be found which might lead to their discovery. The festival proceeded, the fate of Iybcus being still on every tongue. The assembled people were assisting at a dramatic representation, when the dread chorus of the Furies advanced with measured step, and made the circuit of the Theatre. The sound of instruments was heard no more as their choral hymn swelled and rose, thrilling the hearts of all who heard. They sang of the happiness enjoyed by the pure of heart, of the good man whose dwelling was never darkened by their shadow. Then the blood of the listeners grew cold with fear as they told of the vengeance which it was theirs to wreak on the secret murderer, on him whose crime had been vainly hidden from mortal eye. Thus they sang in measured cadence, and passed from view, while a solemn stillness settled on the vast assembly. At this moment a voice was heard from the upper benches, exclaiming, as if in sudden terror, "Behold, comrade! yonder are the cranes of Ibycus!" and a flight of cranes was seen passing directly over the Theatre. The name of the murdered poet caught the ears of the multitude. Each one asked what this exclamation might mean, and what had the cranes to do with him. A cry was raised to seize the man who had spoken, and the one to whom his speech had been addressed. The wretched murderers, thus betrayed by their own guilty fears, confessed the crime, and suffered the punishment they had deserved. Attempts have been made by French and German tragedians, to revive the ancient chorus, but without success, as it is entirely unsuited to the modern drama.

Ques. Were dramatic entertainments as frequent in ancient times as in our own?

Ans. No; but they took place several times in the year, forming a necessary part in the celebration of the principal festivals. The best actors were engaged long beforehand, and were subject to heavy fines if they failed to appear on the appointed day. When such an entertainment was about to take place, the people hastened to the theatre at the dawn of day, that they might secure good seats, as the performance commenced at a very early hour. There were three or four distinct representations during the day, divided by short intervals of repose. During these, the audience walked in the neighboring groves, amused themselves, and partook of the refreshments which they brought with them. When different dramatic poets contended for the prize of excellence, they generally presented two or three pieces each, so that twelve complete dramas were sometimes performed on the same day.

Ques. Were these theatres free to all?

Ans. No; each person was obliged to pay a small sum for admission. When Pericles wished to gain the favor of the Athenians, he reduced the entrance fee to two oboli, and obtained a decree that even this trifling sum should be furnished by the magistrates to the poorer class of citizens. The theatres themselves were erected, and in a great measure maintained at the expense of the state. The cost of the entertainments must have been heavy, if we are to judge by the descriptions given of the scenic arrangements. It is even said that when groves were required, living trees from the forest were planted on the stage.

Whatever may have been the faults of the Greek drama, there is no doubt that it was intended to inculcate principles of religion and morality.

The theatrical entertainments of the Greeks, and their public games, form a striking contrast to the inhuman sports of the Roman amphitheatre.

CHAPTER XLII.

CELEBRATED STATUES.

Ques. What are the most celebrated statues of the heathen divinities?

Ans. The Olympian Jupiter, the Apollo Belvidere, the Diana à la Biche, the Minerva of the Parthenon and the Venus de Medicis.

Ques. What was the Olympian Jupiter?

Ans. This statue, now lost, was forty feet in height, on a pedestal of twelve feet. It was considered the finest work of art of the great Athenian sculptor, Phidias, and there are still in existence busts taken from it, which are remarkable for their calm majesty of expression. The material was what the Greeks called chryselephantine; that is, the flesh was composed of plates of ivory skillfully laid on; but the drapery and ornaments were pure gold. This circumstance is sufficient to account for the destruction of the statue. It was executed for the temple of Jupiter at Olympia, which was worthy of such an adornment, being one of the most magnificent edifices in Greece.

Ques. Describe the Minerva of the Parthenon?

CELEBRATED STATUES. 207

Ans. The statue was of the same dimensions and was composed of the same materials as the Olympian Jupiter; it was also the work of Phidias The Parthenon was one of the most beautiful of the Greek temples, and was enriched by the hand of Phidias with statues and other ornaments. This magnificent temple would have been sufficient in itself to confer immortal glory on the administration of Pericles. It existed in its full beauty for more than a century after his death. It was first despoiled by Lachares, who stripped the statue of Minerva of its golden adornments. It is said he obtained in this manner an amount of precious metal equal to nearly half a million of dollars. The temple itself resisted the attacks of time; it was used successively as a Christian church and a Turkish mosque, and was still entire when the Venetians besieged the citadel of Athens in the year 1687. The Turks converted the Parthenon into a powder magazine; it was unfortunately struck by a bomb, and the entire edifice was reduced to its present ruinous condition. Some of the sculptures and bas-reliefs which once adorned this temple may now be seen in the British Museum. They are called "Elgin Marbles," because they were brought from Greece by Lord Elgin.

Ques. Describe the Venus de Medicis?

Ans. This statue, still perfect, is so called from having been in the possession of the Medicis family. An inscription on its base informs us that it was carved by Cleomenes, an Athenian sculptor, 200 B. C. The artist has succeeded in producing a figure quite perfect in form; but there is nothing spiritual about the Venus, which is, therefore, far inferior to the Jupiter and Minerva.

Ques. Describe the Apollo Belvidere?

Ans. This statue is so called from the Belvidere gallery of the Pope's palace. The artist is unknown, but it is believed to be a Roman work. The god is represented as having just discharged an arrow from his bow against the monster Python. The form and attitude are perfect, but the face is particularly admired for its expression of majesty and power.

Ques. Describe the Diana à la Biche?

Ans. This beautiful statue, now at the Louvre, is considered the counterpart of the Apollo. The goddess is engaged in the chase, and a hind is running by her side. One hand is lifted to draw an arrow from the quiver.

PART II.

CHAPTER I.

Egyptian Divinities.

OSIRIS—APIS—SERAPIS—ISIS -
ANUBIS—HARPOCRATES.

Ques. Who was Osiris?

Ans. Osiris, Apis and Serapis, are three different names of one and the same god. Osiris was the son of Jupiter and of Niobe, the daughter of Phoroneus. He conquered Egypt, which he governed so well and wisely as to receive divine honors from his subjects even during his life. He married, as we have already learned, Iö, the daughter of Inachus, who was more generally known to the Egyptians by the name of Isis.

Osiris was cruelly murdered by his brother Typhon. Isis, after a long search, found his body, which she laid in a monument in an island near Memphis. Osiris became from that time the tutelar deity of the Egyptians. He was regarded as identical with the sun, while Isis was supposed, like Cybele, to personify the earth.

Ques. How was this goddess represented?

Ans. As a woman with the horns of a cow. sometimes, also, as crowned with lotus. Heads of Isis are common among the decorations of Egyptian temples. After the worship of this goddess was introduced into Rome, her image was adorned with different emblems. The mysterious rites of Isis became a cloak for much secret vice, and were repeatedly forbidden at Rome. Tiberius caused the images of the goddess to be thrown into the Tiber; her worship was, however, afterwards revived. The abuses attending it are mentioned with indignation by the poet Juvenal.

Ques. Who was Apis?

Ans. He was the sacred bull of Memphis. The Egyptians maintained that the soul of Osiris passed after death into the body of Apis; and that as often as the sacred animal died, the soul passed into the body of its successor.

Sacrifices were offered to this strange divinity; his birth-day was celebrated with great magnificence, and it was believed that during this festival the crocodiles forgot their usual ferocity, and became harmless. A temple, two chapels, and a court for exercise, were assigned to this god, whose food was always served in vessels of gold. It may be doubted whether the poor animal was capable of appreciating these extraordinary honors; he was not permitted, however, to enjoy them beyond a stated period. If he attained the age of twenty-five years, he was drowned by the attendant priests in the sacred cistern; his body was then carefully embalmed, and buried in the temple of Serapis.

On the death of Apis, whether it occurred in the course of nature or by violence, the whole country was plunged into mourning, which lasted until his successor was found. The animal into whom the divinity had passed, was known by many extraordinary marks; a square white spot on the forehead, the figure of an eagle on the back, a white crescent on the right side, and the mark of a beetle under the tongue. The priests always succeeded in finding an animal with these extraordinary marks, and the happy event was immediately celebrated throughout Egypt.

Ques. How did the people obtain replies from the oracle of Apis?

Ans. By various signs: the votary having proposed a question, offered food to the sacred animal; if he ate, it was considered a favorable omen. It was also a good augury if he entered, of his own accord, a particular stall. When Germanicus offered food to Apis, the animal refused to eat, and this circumstance was afterwards considered as ominous of the early fate of the Roman prince.

Ques. Who was Harpocrates?

Ans. Horus or Harpocrates was the son of Osiris. He was worshipped as the god of Silence, and is represented as a boy, seated on a lotus-flower, with his finger on his lips.

Besides the gods we have mentioned, the Egyptians worshipped the dog, the wolf, the crocodile, the ibis, and many other animals. They even attributed divinity to certain plants and roots. Juvenal, in one of his Satires, thus ridicules their superstition:

> Who has not heard where Egypt's realms are nam'd
> What monster gods her frantic sons have fram'd?
> Here Ibis gorged with well-grown serpents, there
> The Crocodile commands religious fear;
> Where Memnon's statue magic strains inspire
> With vocal sounds that emulate the lyre;
> And Thebes, such, Fate, are thy disastrous turns,
> Now prostrate o'er her pompous ruins mourns ·
> A monkey-god, prodigious to be told!
> Strikes the beholder's eye with burnish'd gold:
> To godship here blue Triton's scaly herd,
> The river progeny is there preferr'd:
> Through towns Diana's power neglected lies,
> Where to her dogs aspiring temples rise!
> And should you leeks or onions eat, no time
> Would expiate the sacrilegious crime.
> Religious nations sure, and blest abodes,
> Where every orchard is o'er-run with gods

CHAPTER II.

EASTERN MYTHOLOGY.

Deities of the Assyrians.

BAAL, OR BEL—MOLOCH.

Ques. Who were these divinities?

Ans. The names Baal and Moloch seem to have been, at first, different appellations of the Sun; later they assumed another signification, and were applied to distinct deities.

Ques. Where was the Sun worshipped under the name of Baal of Bel (the Lord)?

Ans. In Babylon. The famous tower of Babel or Belus, was there devoted to his worship, although the highest apartment of the edifice served also as an observatory, and was the repository of the most ancient astronomical observations. Some writers have imagined that the Chaldeans and Babylonians worshipped Nimrod under the name of Belus, but it is generally believed that with these nations, and the ancient Canaanites, this was one of the many appellations of the Sun.

Ques. What proof have we of the popularity of this god among the Phœnicians and Carthaginians?

Ans. In their proper names; as among the former, Eth*baal*, Jerub*baal*; among the latter, Hanni*bal*, Asdru*baal*.

Ques. By whom was the worship of Baal introduced among the Israelites?

Ans. By King Achab or Ahab. They offered human sacrifices to Baal in groves, or high places, and on the terraces of their houses. Jeremias reproaches the Jews with building "the high places of Baalim, to burn their children with fire for a holocaust to Baalim." This text shows the extent to which the apostate Hebrews carried this abominable worship.

MOLOCH.

Ques. Who was Moloch?

Ans. He was a divinity of the Ammonites. The Phœnicians were also particularly devoted to his worship. Young children and infants were offered as holocausts to this cruel god. These horrid sacrifices were most frequent in Carthage. When the Sicilian Agathocles threatened that city, we are told that five hundred infants, many the first-born of noble parents, were consumed in one day on the altar of Moloch.

Ques. How was this god represented?

Ans. By a brazen image, which was so con

trived that when a child was laid upon its extended arms, they were lowered, and the little victim immediately fell into the fiery furnace placed at the foot of the idol.

Ques. Was Moloch worshipped by the Jews?

Ans. Yes; it would seem that they were addicted to this idolatry before their departure from Egypt, since Moses in many places forbids the Israelites, under pain of death, to dedicate their children to Moloch, by passing them through fire. Solomon built a temple for his worship on the Mount of Olives. Later human sacrifices were offered to him in the valley of Hinnom, called also Tophet, which lay to the east of Jerusalem.

Ques. Where does Milton refer to this god?

Ans. Assuming that the demons or fallen angels received the worship of men, under the names of different heathen divinities, he thus describes Moloch amid the host of Satan:

"First, Moloch, horrid king, besmear'd with blood
Of human sacrifice, and parents' tears;
Though, for the noise of drums and timbrels loud,
Their children's cries unheard, that passed through fire,
To his grim idol. Him the Ammonite
Worshipp'd in Rabba and her watery plain,
In Argob and in Basan, to the stream
Of utmost Arnon; nor content with such
Audacious neighborhood, the wisest heart
Of Solomon he led by fraud to build
His temple right against the temple of God,
On that opprobrious hill: and made his grove
The pleasant valley of Hinnom, Tophet thence
And black Gehenna call'd, the type of Hell."

Ques. Who was Astaroth?

Ans. This goddess, called by the Greeks Astarte, represented the moon, in the same manner as Baal was held to be identical with the sun. The Hebrews always connected the worship of these two divinities. According to Cicero, Astarte was the Syrian Venus, and it is certain that in her worship, and the festivals celebrated in her honor, there is some foundation for this idea. While human sacrifices were offered to Baal, wheaten cakes, wine and perfumes were laid upon the altar of Astaroth.

Notwithstanding these more innocent offerings, her worship was rendered infamous by the license which prevailed during these festivals, and the open immorality practised by her votaries.

THAMMUZ.

Ques. Who was Thammuz?

Ans. This was another name for Adonis, whose story is of Eastern origin. His death, which we have already referred to in connection with the goddess Venus, is said to have taken place in the mountains of Libanus, from which the river Adonis flows to the sea. The Assyrian women mourned for him in the autumn-time. It was believed that at this season the river changed its color, and ran red, as if tinged with blood. To this Milton alludes:

> "Thammuz came next behind,
> Whose annual wound in Lebanon allured
> The Syrian damsels to lament his fate
> In amorous ditties all a summer's day;
> While smooth Adonis from his native rock
> Ran purple to the sea, supposed with blood
> Of Thammuz yearly wounded."

The prophet Ezekiel, in relating the iniquities committed in Jerusalem, says that he saw women sitting by the north gate of the temple, who mourned for Adonis. (In the Hebrew, Thammuz.)

OANNES.

Ques. Who was Oannes?

Ans. He was a god of the Assyrians, half man, half fish, who was said to dwell in the sea, from which he came at stated times, to instruct the Babylonians in wisdom and science. Oannes is the Dagon of the Philistines.

CHAPTER III.

PERSIA.

Ques. What was the religion of the ancient Persians?

Ans. We derive our knowledge of their religion principally from their Zend-avesta, or Sacred Book.

Ques. What does the Zend-avesta contain?

Ans. The doctrines of Zoroaster, an Eastern sage, who is thought to have lived in Bactria about twelve hundred years before our era.

Ques. Was the Zend-avesta written by Zoroaster?

Ans. But a small portion, if any, of the Sacred Books were written by him, but the most ancient passages, which are in verse, were probably written soon after his time, when the knowledge of his doctrines was still preserved. The Parsees, or modern followers of Zoroaster, now scattered through India, say that the Zend-avesta formerly consisted of twenty-one books, but that the greater part were lost in the troubled times that followed the conquest of Persia by Alexander the Great.

Ques. What is the form of the Zend-avesta?

Ans. It is in the form of a dialogue, in which Ormuzd, the supreme deity, replies to the inquiries of Zoroaster, and teaches him his will with regard to his creatures.

Ques. What were the doctrines of Zoroaster?

Ans. This philosopher was more enlightened than his contemporaries, and was probably acquainted with primitive tradition. He taught the existence of one supreme Being called "the Eternal," who created two other mighty beings, and imparted to them a portion of his own eternal divinity.

Ques. Who were these deities?

Ans. Ormuzd, or Oromasdes, who remained faithful and pure, governs the world with all the attributes which are given to the true God. Ahriman, on the contrary, uses all his energies for evil; and is, in all respects, considered as a sort of independent demon, endowed with infinite and untiring malice.

Ques. What part did each of these divinities take in the creation?

Ans. Ormuzd created men and angels, the sun, moon and stars, and everything which can contribute to the welfare or pleasure of his creatures. Ahriman created the wild beasts, poisonous serpents, etc., and sent diseases, earthquakes and storms. The Persians thus believed in two independent principles, one of good, and one of evil, but they worshipped only the first.

Ques. Did they not worship the sun?

Ans. They probably did in later times, but the early followers of Zoroaster reverenced the sun and fire as emblems of Ormuzd. Perpetual fire was kept burning on their altars. The Parsees of Hindostan say that they have sacred fire which has never been extinguished since the time of Zoroaster. All the sacred fires were originally lit from that which Zoroaster brought from heaven. The Guebres, as these people are sometimes called, often built their temples over subterranean fires.

Ques. Is there any such fire now reverenced by them?

Ans. Yes, near the town of Bakoo in Georgia, on the Caspian Sea, there is a perpetual flame issuing from a limestone rock. It is watched by priests, and is much venerated by the surrounding tribes. Pilgrimages are made to this sacred fire from all parts of Asia.

Ques. What is the cause of this phenomenon?

Ans. Bakoo and the surrounding country abound in naphtha and petroleum. The sacred fire is simply a jet of inflammable gas escaping from the rocks, which, once lit, burns perpetually, as the supply is inexhaustible.

Ques. Were the Persians attached to magical arts?

Ans. Yes, their priests mingled the fables of astrology with their astronomical learning; hence, from the word magi, is derived our word magician.

Ques. Where did the Persians offer their sacrifices?

Ans. Generally on the tops of lofty mountains

Ques. When was the religion of Zoroaster suppressed in Persia?

Ans. After the conquest of Persia, by the Arabs, which took place in the seventh century, those who refused to embrace the Koran fled to Hindostan, where they still exist under the name of Parsees. At Bombay they are an active intelligent and wealthy class.

CHAPTER IV.

Hindoo Mythology.

BRAHMA—THE VEDAS

Ques. What are the Vedas?

Ans. The Vedas are the Sacred Books of the Hindoos, and are much reverenced by them. They maintain that they were composed by Brahma, the Supreme Deity, at the creation.

Ques. When do the Hindoos think that the world was created?

Ans. At an incredibly remote period; they say the present arrangement of the Vedas was made by a sage named Vyasa, some five thousand years ago.

Ques. What is the more correct opinion?

Ans. That they were written in the second thousand years before our era, a little later, probably, than the Books of Moses.

Ques. Had the Hindoos then conquered the country which now bears their name?

Ans. No; they were only crossing the borders of India.

Ques. In what form are the Vedas written?

Ans. In poetry. The principal Veda contains ten thousand double verses. These works are heavy and uninteresting, but very important to historians.

Ques. Why so?

Ans. Because they throw light on the early history of the Indian and European races.

Ques. What do the Vedas teach of God?

Ans. They teach one supreme deity, called Brahma, and like the Persians seem to have some idea of the Trinity, speaking of Brahma, Vishnu, and Siva, as one God. The modern Hindoos, however, worship them as distinct divinities

Ques. What are the offices of these gods?

Ans. Brahma created all things, Vishnu preserves them, and when the end of the world is come, which the Vedas say will occur in about twelve million years, Siva will destroy them.

Ques. What is there peculiar in the history of Vishnu?

Ans. His Avatars, or incarnations, which are numerous, but ten are more especially celebrated.

Ques. What was the first Avatar?

Ans. The first Avatar was when Vishnu assumed the form of a fish, and saved Manu, the father of the human race, from a universal deluge.

Ques. What is the ninth Avatar?

Ans. In the ninth Avatar, Vishnu appeared in the form of Krishna, a sort of Indian Apollo; the last of the Sacred Books is that which contains the life of Krishna.

Ques. What is there remarkable about this life?

Ans. So many circumstances closely resemble corresponding events in the life of our Saviour, that it is impossible the coincidence should be accidental. It is supposed this book was written after our era by some one who had heard imperfect accounts of the life of our Lord.

Ques. What is to be the tenth Avatar?

Ans. The tenth Avatar is called Kalki, in which Vishnu will come to judge the world, destroying the wicked and rewarding the good.

Ques. What do you say of Siva?

Ans. Siva, or Mahadeva, as he is more generally called, has a vast number of followers. His worshippers and those of Vishnu form two distinct sects. Brahma, having finished his work, has but one temple in India. It is doubtful whether the worshippers of Juggernaut belong to the sect of Vishnu, or of Siva.

Ques. What do the Hindoos believe of the soul?

Ans. They think that every soul is a part of Brahma, as a spark is a part of the fire, and that finally all souls will be absorbed into Brahma, as drops of water are lost in the ocean. They also believe in metempsychosis.

Ques. What is metempsychosis?

Ans. The transmigration of souls. The Hindoos believe that if a man lead a pure life, his soul will pass, after death, into another human body, but that if he has been wicked, it will enter into the body of some unclean animal. They think the soul will transmigrate many times before being finally united to Brahma. This belief makes many of the Hindoos afraid to kill animals for food, lest they may possess human souls, and be perhaps their own friends or relations.

Ques. What are Castes?

Ans. They are different classes into which the Hindoos have been divided from the earliest times.

Ques. How many castes are there?

Ans. Four; the Brahmins or priests, who sprung from the head of Brahma; the Warrior caste, which issued from his arms; the Agriculturists and Traders, who came from his thighs, and lastly, the Sudras, or laborers, who sprung from his feet.

Ques. Is there much distinction between the castes?

Ans. Yes; they cannot under any circumstances intermarry; nor can a member of a lower caste ever pass to a higher. Only, if he lead a good life, he may console himself with the hope of being born in a higher caste the next time.

Ques. Is there any caste lower than the Sudras?

Ans. No regular caste, but there exists a most unhappy race called Pariahs, who are treated with the utmost contempt, and employed only in the vilest offices. They cannot enter the house of any one belonging to a pure caste, and they are not only unclean themselves, but are supposed to contaminate everything they touch. Different accounts are given as to the origin of these Pariahs.

Ques. Are the Hindoos allowed to eat flesh?

Ans. The three higher castes are forbidden it altogether. The Sudras may eat every kind but beef, but the Pariahs are under no restriction whatever. The idea seems to be that they are so vile that no kind of food could pollute them.

Ques. Are the castes ancient?

Ans. So much so, that it is impossible to say when they were first established. The Pariahs are being gradually raised from their degradation by the efforts of Christian missionaries.

BUDDHA.

Ques. Who was Buddha?

Ans. Buddha is said by the Vedas to have been a delusive incarnation of Vishnu, but his followers give a different account.

Ques. What do they say?

Ans. They say that he was a mortal sage, called Guatama, and also Buddha, or the Wise.

Ques. When did Buddha live?

Ans. We cannot ascertain exactly, but it is probable he was a contemporary of Solomon—that is, he lived about one thousand years before our era. He was the son of a king, and was distinguished by wisdom, virtue and every personal gift. He was so disgusted with the wickedness of men, that he retired into a desert place, where he spent six years in prayer and meditation. At the end of this time, he began his career as a religious teacher. He preached first in Benares, but his doctrines were received with so much favor that he lived to see them spread over all India. Buddha died at the age of eighty.

Ques. Was Buddhism tolerated by the Brahmins?

Ans. It appears that for several centuries it was, and that it extended to Ceylon, and the Eastern peninsula.

Ques. What are the doctrines of the Buddhists?

Ans. They reject the Vedas altogether, and the religious observances prescribed in them. They allow animal food, and acknowledge no distinction of castes. Bloody sacrifices are prohibited. One of the duties of a priest of Buddha is to study the medicinal properties of plants in order to benefit his fellow men. We may see, therefore, that Buddha had more reasonable and humane ideas than those who composed the Vedas, and that he was probably a true sage among his people.

Ques. Is Buddhism common in India?

Ans. No; after being tolerated for a long time, a fierce and continued persecution was raised against it. This had the effect of suppressing the sect almost entirely in India, and of spreading it in the adjacent countries.

Ques. When was the worship of Buddha first introduced into China?

Ans. About the year 65 of our era. From China it spread to Corea, Japan and Java.

In Japan, Buddhism has, to a great extent, supplanted the Sinto religion, the ancient faith of Japan. The word Sinto signifies spirit worship; the priests of this sect teach that the world is governed by an infinite number of spirits. The chief of these animates the sun; others rule the moon, stars, and different elements.

The worship of the sun is the most important exterior part of their religion, and the Japanese were so much attached to this form of idolatry, that the Buddhists have incorporated it with their own rites.

CHAPTER V.

CHINA.

Ques Is Buddhism universally followed in China?

Ans. There is, strictly speaking, no state or national religion in China, but all forms of worship are tolerated, unless they are considered politically dangerous. Among the pagan Chinese three principal religions are admitted, which are now considered equally good, although there were formerly bitter wars between their followers.

Ques. What are these?

Ans. The first, of which Confucius is in some sort the founder, is called the "Doctrine of the Lettered;" the second is regarded by its professors as the primitive religion of the ancient inhabitants of China. The priests are called Tao-sse, or Doctors of Reason, from the principal doctrine of their great teacher, Lao-tze, who considered primordial reason as the creator of all things. The third religion is Buddhism, which, as we have seen, was introduced into China in the first century of our era.

Ques. Who was Confucius?

Ans. Confucius is the Latinized name of a philosopher whom the Chinese call Kung-fu-tse, (Reverend Master Kung). He was born in the year 551 B. C., and died in 479; eleven years before Socrates was born. Confucius was carefully educated in virtue and learning by his widowed mother. At her death he retired, according to Chinese custom, for the appointed three years of mourning. During this time, he devoted himself to the study of ancient writers, and noticing how completely the morality of the old sages was forgotten in China, he determined to restore their usages and doctrines. After careful preparation, he set himself up as a teacher, and his disciples were soon numbered by tens of thousands. Confucius travelled through the neighboring countries, preaching wherever he went; he was at one time prime minister of the empire, but his last years were spent in retirement with some chosen disciples. We read that he paid a visit to Lao-tze, and was so confounded by the sublime wisdom of that philosopher, that on his return home he remained three days buried in profound thought, refusing to speak, or answer any of the questions put to him by his disciples. Confucius enjoyed unbounded popularity during life, but the honors paid to him after death, have no parallel in history. His tablet is in every school in China, and both master and pupils are required to prostrate themselves before it at the beginning and end of each class. Every town has a temple erected in his honor, and his statue is to be found in every literary institution. Confucius left one grandson, Tse-tse, whose descendants constitute the only hereditary nobility in China. In the seventeenth century, they numbered eleven thousand males.

Ques. What were the doctrines of Confucius?

Ans. This philosopher did not originate any religious creed: he was simply a teacher of morality. It is thought, from many passages in his writings, that he believed in one Omnipotent God. He does not, however, inculcate any such doctrine, nor does he ever speak of any future reward as a motive for virtuous actions. Filial piety and other social and domestic virtues are strongly inculcated. It would be well for the Chinese of the present day, if their conduct corresponded to the maxims of their great teacher, whose morality, though often defective, contains much that is to be admired. It is a proof, if any were needed, that human motives are too weak to have any lasting influence on the passions of men; and the Chinese, particularly the followers of Confucius, seem to have lost even the last traces of natural religion.

Ques. Why then do they persevere in his worship?

Ans. The honors paid to Confucius, as well as to the souls of their ancestors, constitute an external religion for official persons and literary men.

There seems to be no sort of belief connected with these observances.

Ques. What difficulties did this cause among the Christian missionaries?

Ans. Some of these missionaries believed that the honors paid to Confucius were purely civil observances; and that the worship of the souls of deceased relations, the oblations made at their tombs, etc., were simply national customs to which no superstitious idea was attached. As they were assured of this by the most learned men of the Empire, they permitted the newly converted Chinese to continue these observances. Others, however, considered that, among the ignorant, these rites always degenerated into superstition, and often into idolatry. The dispute was referred to Rome, and after a careful inquiry, the latter opinion prevailed; the rites in honor of Confucius, together with the worship of ancestors, were forbidden to the Chinese Christians.

Ques. Who was Lao-tze?

Ans. He was a Chinese philosopher, contemporary with Confucius. With regard to his life and actions, many absurd and impossible things are related. His name, Lao-tze, means 'Old Child;' and the Chinese say this appellation was given him because he was born already old, and with gray hair. The followers of Lao-tze believe in a spiritual world, in spiritual manifestations, and in the transmigration of souls. This doctrine is called the religion of Tao, or Reason. The priests are now only cheats and jugglers, living on the superstition of the people, to whom they sell charms and spells.

Notwithstanding the degraded character of his followers, the writings of Lao-tze prove that he was a true sage, a man of noble and elevated ideas. He has been compared favorably with Plato, and some have claimed that the Chinese philosopher travelled as far west as Athens. Be this as it may, it is certain Lao-tze spent some time in Persia and Syria. The Ten Tribes had just been dispersed over Asia by the conquests of Salmanasar; and it is not possible that a sage so eager in the pursuit of religious knowledge, should have failed to learn something of the ancient prophecies and the Mosaic law.

Ques. What did Lao-tze teach with regard to God?

Ans. In his writings he declares plainly that the world was erected by a threefold divinity. His followers, however, like the rest of the Chinese, have no definite idea of God.

Ques. What class of Chinese follow the doctrines of Buddha, or Fo?

Ans. At present the Chinese Buddhists belong principally to the lower classes. Formerly this religion was in higher repute, but the magnificent temples of Buddha are now going gradually to decay, and there seems no prospect that any attempt will be made to restore them. The Bonzes, or Buddhist priests, are ignorant and degraded, and are allowed to live in the greatest poverty. They are not permitted to marry; to keep up their numbers they buy young children, who may be had in China for a few sapecks, and these are trained for the service of Buddha. These Bonzes have sunk so low in public estimation, that they are often hired to perform inferior parts on the stage.

Ques. Where is the most celebrated temple of Buddha?

Ans. In Pou-tou, an island in the Archipelago of Chusan. This temple retains many traces of its former magnificence, and is particularly remarkable for a triple statue of Buddha. There are three gigantic figures, richly gilt, which represent the divinity in the past, the present and the future. In this temple is a hall dedicated to the Goddess of Porcelain, and every part of the edifice is crowded with hideous idols of the lesser divinities.

Ques. What is the general feeling of the Chinese on religious subjects?

Ans. They are entirely indifferent, and have but a vague idea of the existence of anything beyond the present life. This indifference is the greatest obstacle with which the Christian missionaries have to contend in China.

Ques. Do the Chinese ever argue among themselves on points of belief?

Ans. Never. When Chinese, who are strangers

to each other, meet, a polite formula is to ask "To what sublime religion do you belong?" Then one will call himself a Buddhist, another a follower of Confucius, etc., upon which politeness requires that each one should speak slightingly of his own religion, and praise the sect to which he does not belong. These compliments end by all repeating in chorus a proverbial phrase to the effect that all men are brothers, and religions are of no consequence.

Ques. If such total indifference prevails in China, on the subject of religion, how does it happen that Christianity should be so severely persecuted?

Ans. This arises partly from the political fears of the Chinese government, and its jealousy of strangers. The missionaries are, of course, foreigners, and it is natural that the emperors should imagine them to be working in the interest of the great western nations whose power they so much fear. There are other reasons; the purity of Christian morals has been always a reproach to pagan society, and the spirit of darkness never fails to rouse the prejudices and passions of men against the progress of the faith. In ancient Rome, where the idols and superstitions of every conquered nation found a ready welcome, Christianity obtained a foothold only after three centuries of persecution.

CHAPTER VI.

Thibet.

THE GRAND LAMA

Ques. What is the prevailing religion of Thibet?

Ans. Buddhism prevails in Thibet and Tartary. The people of these countries are more thoughtful than the Chinese, and more earnest with regard to religious matters. Their priests, called Lamas, live together in large communities. They are given to study, and their dwellings, or Lamaseries, often contain large and valuable libraries. Many of the Lamas are addicted to demon worship and sorcery, but these are generally looked upon with aversion by the more virtuous among their brethren.

Ques. Who is the Grand Lama?

Ans. He is a sort of High Priest of Buddhism residing in Lassa, the capital of Thibet; he is invested with an entirely supernatural character.

Ques. How is this?

Ans. The Buddhists believe that the confinement of the soul in a human body is a state of misery, and the punishment of sins committed in a former state of existence. They maintain, however, that pure spirits, from time to time, assume our human nature voluntarily, in order to promote the welfare of mankind. Such are the Lamas, and since the victories of Genghis Kan in the East, the Lama residing in Thibet has been considered the Chief Pontiff of his sect, and a perpetual incarnation of Buddha. He is also a temporal sovereign, although he is controlled by the Chinese government.

Ques. How is the line perpetuated?

Ans. When the Lama dies, his soul enters immediately into the body of some child, so that he is simply said to transmigrate.

Ques. How is the child discovered?

Ans. This is an affair of some difficulty, but the inferior Lamas always succeed in finding the hidden divinity. The child into whom they supposed the Lama's soul has entered, is required to remember the most private acts of the Lama's life, to recognize, as familiar objects, the articles which he was accustomed to use, etc. The children thus examined have sometimes answered in so extraordinary a manner that many have supposed Satan was permitted to aid in the imposture.

CHAPTER VII.

MYTHOLOGY OF SCANDINAVIA.

Ques. What does this mythology include?

Ans. The ancient superstitions of that portion of Northern Europe now known as Sweden, Norway, Denmark and Iceland.

Ques. What is the general character of Scandinavian mythology?

Ans. It has none of the grace and poetic beauty which characterize the fables of Greece and Rome; and it differs equally from the more mystical superstitions of the Persians and Hindoos. In warm and fertile regions, the temper, even of the barbarian, is softened into harmony with the scenes around him, and his superstitions, though still sensual, are more gentle and refined. On the other hand, the wild and rugged North made its own impress on the Scandinavian tribes, and their superstitions were gloomy and extravagant, with sometimes an element of savage grandeur and sublimity.

Ques. Was this mythology transmitted by oral tradition only?

Ans. This must have been the case for a long time; as the oldest of the Eddas was compiled only in the eleventh century, and the stories which it contains of the Northern gods and heroes, had been long familiar to the people in the recitations of their bards. The Scandinavian Skalds or bards were, like the Celtic, historians as well as minstrels.

Ques. Who composed the Eddas?

Ans. It is impossible to say. The oldest, or poetic Edda, was compiled by Sâmund Sigfûsson, an Icelandic priest, about the middle of the eleventh century. He was educated in France and Germany, and spent some time in Rome before his return to Iceland. He was induced to compile the Edda, principally, it would seem, from a patriotic desire of preserving the ancient legends of his race. The word Edda means ancestress, and it is so called because it is considered the mother of Icelandic poetry. The Sagas were written in Denmark and the Scandinavian peninsula.

Ques. What account do the Eddas give of the creation?

Ans. They say that in the beginning, there was neither heaven nor earth, but a world of mist, in which flowed a mysterious fountain. Twelve rivers issued from this fountain, and when they had flowed far from their source, froze into ice, which, gradually accumulating, the great deep was filled up. Southward from the world of mist, was the world of light. From this a warm wind flowed upon the ice, and melted it. The vapors rose in the air and formed clouds, from which sprung the Frost Giant and his progeny; also the cow Audhumbla, by whose milk the giant was nourished. The Frost Giants were the enemies of gods and men. From the ice of the lower deep a god arose, who married a daughter of the giants, and became the father of three sons, Odin, Vili and Ve. These slew the giant Ymir, and out of his body formed the earth on which we live. His bones were changed into mountains, his hair into trees; of his skull they made the heavens, and of his brain, clouds charged with hail and snow. Odin next regulated the days and seasons by placing the sun and moon in the heavens, and appointing them their respective courses. As soon as the sun shed its rays upon the earth, the plants and trees began to bud and sprout. The three gods walked by the side of the sea, admiring their new creation, but seeing that it was uninhabited, they resolved to create man. Aske and Embla, the first man and woman, were therefore formed, the man out of an ash, and the woman out of an alder. They were the parents of the whole human race.

Ques. What idea had the ancient Scandinavians of the form of the earth?

Ans. Their notions on the subject were childish in the extreme. They thought that the ash tree Ygdrasill, supported the entire universe. This tree had three roots, one of which extended into

Asgard, the dwelling-place of the gods; another into Jotunheim, the abode of the giants; and a third into Niffleheim, the region of darkness and cold. Under the tree lies Ymir, and his efforts to throw off the weight cause earthquakes. The root that extends into Asgard is carefully tended by three Norns, who correspond to the Fates of Greek mythology. Asgard could only be entered by crossing the bridge Bifrost, (the rainbow).

Ques. Describe Asgard.

Ans. It contained gold and silver palaces, the dwellings of the gods, but the most famous and beautiful of these was Valhalla, the residence of Odin. This god is represented as seated on a throne which overlooks all heaven and earth. On his shoulders sit the ravens, Hugin and Munin, who fly every day over the whole world, and on their return report to him all that they have seen. At Odin's feet lie two wolves, to whom he gives all the meat that is set before him, as he himself stands in no need of food. Mead is for him both food and drink.

Ques. How is Odin's name sometimes written?

Ans. Woden; and from this comes the name of the fourth day of the week, Woden's day, changed to Wednesday.

Ques. Has Odin any other name?

Ans. He was sometimes called Alfadur, (All father,) but this name is occasionally used in a way that seems to prove that the Scandinavians had an idea of a divinity superior to Odin, Un-created and Eternal.

Ques. What were the delights of Valhalla, and who were permitted to enjoy them?

Ans. None were admitted to Valhalla but heroes who had fallen in battle. Women, children, and all who had died a peaceful death, were excluded as unworthy. The joys of Valhalla consisted in eating, drinking and fighting. They feasted on the flesh of the boar Schrimnir, which was cooked every day, and became whole again every night. The goat Heidrun supplied them with never-failing draughts of mead, which they drank from the skulls of their slaughtered enemies. For pastime, they fought, and cut one another to pieces. When the hour of feasting came, they recovered from their wounds, and were whole as before.

THOR.

Ques. Who was Thor?

Ans. He was Odin's eldest son, and was god of thunder. His mighty strength depended upon three things—his hammer, his belt of strength, and his iron gloves. The giants at one time obtained his hammer, and he was obliged to use a very singular stratagem to recover it.

Ques. What was this?

Ans. Thor was most anxious to recover his hammer, but the giant Thrym had buried it eight fathoms deep under the rocks of Jotunheim. Loki undertook to negotiate with Thrym; but the giant demanded the hand of the goddess Freya, and refused to restore the hammer on any other terms. Thor was much troubled, as he knew how vain it was to expect that the bright goddess of love and song would consent to dwell in the dismal regions of Jotunheim. The artful Loki proposed that Thor should array himself in the garments of Freya, and accompany him to the abode of the Frost Giants. Thor consented, and Thrym welcomed his veiled bride with great joy, attributing her silence to a modest reserve. He was much surprised, however, to see her eat for supper eight salmons, besides a full grown ox and other delicacies, washing down the repast with proportionate draughts of mead. Loki bade him not to wonder at this, as her thoughts had been so much occupied by her approaching nuptials that she had not eaten for many days. When Thrym was startled by the fiery eyes he saw gleaming from beneath the bridal veil, Loki again made an excuse which satisfied him, so he brought the hammer, and laid it on the lap of the supposed bride. Thor seized the weapon, and finding his wonted strength restored, he threw off his disguise, and rushed upon Thrym, whom he slew with all his followers.

Loki had served Thor in this adventure; on another occasion he incurred his wrath by an injury offered to Sif or Sifa, his wife. The hair of this goddess flowed around her in sunny waves that shone like gold. She was proud of this adornment; and Loki, willing to punish her vanity, and always ready for mischief, found means to cut off her hair while she slept.

The goddess was inconsolable, and Thor sought the insolent offender, intending to crush him with his redoubtable hammer.

Loki was terrified, and sought the dwelling of the Gnomes. These skillful workmen gave him a head of hair which they had spun from the purest gold, and which was so wonderfully wrought that it would attach itself to the head of the wearer, and increase in length like ordinary hair. Sifa was enchanted with the golden locks, and the cunning Loki escaped the threatened punishment.

From Thor's name is derived the word Thursday.

FREY AND FREYA.

Ques. Who was Frey?

Ans. He was one of the greatest of the gods. He presided over rain, sunshine, and the fruits of the earth. From his name comes our word Friday.

Ques. Who was Freya?

Ans. She was the sister of Frey or Freyr. She loved music, Spring and flowers, and was a friend of the elves, or good fairies. Freya was invoked by lovers, and seems to have been a sort of Scandinavian Venus.

BRAGI.

Ques. Who was Bragi?

Ans. He was god of poetry, but he scorned all lighter strains, and was the patron of those only who sung the praises of the gods and the deeds of warriors.

Iduna, his wife, kept in a casket certain apples which the gods, when they felt age approaching, had only to taste to renew the vigor and bloom of youth. On the approach of the Great Twilight, and the end of time, this fruit was to lose its magic power.

HEIMDALL

Ques. Who was Heimdall?

Ans. He was the watchman of the gods, and was stationed at the extreme verge of heaven to guard the bridge Bifrost. The gods continually feared that the giants might force their way over the shining arch, and invade Valhalla.

Heimdall required less sleep than a bird, and his sight was so keen that he could distinguish the smallest object, for a thousand leagues around, even in the darkest night. His quickness of hearing was equally wonderful; he could hear the wool growing on the sheep's backs, and the grain sprouting in the fields. He possessed a horn of such construction that when he blew upon it, the sound spread in widening circles until it reached the uttermost confines of the world. Heimdall was not permitted to marry, lest any care for wife or children might interrupt his unceasing watchfulness.

VIDAR.

Ques. Who was Vidar?

Ans. He was the god of silence. His strength was almost equal to that of Thor; he was often employed like Mercury as messenger of the gods. He had sandals which sustained him equally in the air, and upon the water.

HODUR.

Ques. Who was Hodur?

Ans. He was a blind deity, endowed with prodigious strength. He was mild and benevolent, but certain terrible predictions concerning him inspired such terror in Asgard that it was not lawful for any god to pronounce his name. Hodur seems to have been a personification of night.

THE VALKYRIOR.

Ques. Who are the Valkyrior?

Ans. According to the Scandinavian tradition, they are warlike virgins, the messengers of Odin, and their name signifies "Choosers of the slain." Odin is desirous of collecting a great many heroes in Valhalla, that he may be able to meet the giants in the final contest at the end of the world. He sends the Valkyrior, therefore, to every battle field to make choice of those who shall be slain. When they ride forth on their errand, mounted upon war steeds and in full armor, their shields and helmets shed a strange flickering light, which flashes up over the northern skies, and is called by men, "Aurora Borealis," or "Northern Lights."

LOKI AND HIS PROGENY.

Ques. Who was Loki?

Ans. Loki was an evil deity, the contriver of all fraud and mischief. He was very handsome, but of fickle and malicious temper. Loki had three children, the wolf Fenris, the Midgard serpent, and Hela, or Death. The gods were not ignorant that these monsters were growing up, and would one day bring much evil upon gods and men. Odin, therefore, sent a messenger to bring them to him. When they came, he threw the serpent into the deep ocean by which the earth is surrounded. The monster soon grew to such an enormous size, that, holding his tail in his mouth, he encircled the whole world. Hela was cast into Nifleheim, where she receives as her subjects all who die of sickness or old age. The wolf Fenris gave the gods much trouble before they succeeded in chaining him. He broke the strongest fetters as if they were made of cobwebs. Finally, the mountain spirits fashioned a chain which he could not break. It was fabricated of the roots of stones, the noise made by the footfall of a cat, and other equally absurd and imaginary material.

BALDUR THE GOOD

Ques. Who was Baldur?

Ans. He was the son of Odin, good and exceedingly beautiful. He was tormented by terrible dreams, indicating that his life was in peril. He told these things to the assembled gods, who resolved to do all in their power to protect him. Frigga, the wife of Odin, exacted an oath from the elements, fire, air, water, and from everything animate and inanimate upon the earth—stones, plants, rocks and animals—that they would do no harm to Baldur. The gods were so well satisfied with this, that they amused themselves with throwing sticks, stones and all manner of weapons at the hero, who was not harmed by anything. Loki, with his usual malice, was determined on Baldur's death, but did not know exactly how to bring it about. He assumed, therefore, the form of an old woman, and went to see Frigga. The goddess asked him what the gods were doing at their meetings. The disguised Loki replied that they were throwing darts and stones at Baldur, without being able to hurt him.

He inquired of Frigga, in his turn, if it were really true that she had exacted an oath of all created things, to spare Baldur. "Aye," said Frigga; "all things have sworn, save a mistletoe which was growing on a mountain side, and which I thought too young and feeble to crave an oath from." As soon as Loki heard this, he went away rejoicing. Having cut down the mistletoe, he repaired to the place where the gods were assembled, and put the bough among the sticks which they were casting in sport at Baldur. It was thrown with the rest, and Baldur fell to the ground pierced through and through. The gods were overwhelmed with grief, and broke forth in the wildest lamentations. Then Frigga came, and asked, who among them would show his love for her, and for Baldur, by procuring the deliverance of the hero. Not having fallen in battle, Baldur had passed into the power of Hela, who ruled over the gloomy regions of Hell, or Niffleheim. Hermod, the son of Odin, offered to repair thither, and pay to Hela a mignty ransom for the return of his brother Baldur. He set out, therefore, mounted on Odin's horse Sleipnir, which had eight legs and could outstrip the wind. For nine days, and as many nights, the hero rode through darksome glens where no object could be discerned in the gloom. On the tenth, he came to a dark river, which was spanned by a bridge of gold; this was the entrance into Hell, and Hermod rode over it fearlessly, although it shook and swayed under his living weight. He passed the night in discourse with Baldur, and the next morning preferred his petition to Hela. He offered any ransom she might name for Baldur's return, assuring her that heaven and earth resounded with lamentations for the hero. Hela would take no ransom, but wished to try if Baldur were really so beloved. "If," said she, "all things in the world, both living and lifeless, weep for him, then shall he return; but if any one thing refuse to weep for him, then shall he be kept in Hell."

On hearing the result of Hermod's mission, the gods made proclamation throughout the world, beseeching all created things to weep for Baldur's deliverance. All complied with this request; both men and animals, all, even to the savage beasts of the forest, shed tears for the hero. The trees and plants shed crystal drops like rain, and even the rocks and stones were covered with a glittering dew. One old hag only, sat in a cavern, and refused to weep, saying.

> "Thankt will wail
> With dry tears
> Baldur's bale-fire.
> Let Hela keep her own."

It was strongly suspected that this hag was no other than Loki himself, who never ceased to work evil among gods and men. Thus Baldur was prevented from coming back to Asgard.

Funeral of Baldur.

Ques. How was the hero buried?
Ans. Baldur's body was borne to the seashore, and placed upon a funeral pile which was built of his own ship, the largest in the world. All the gods were present, and even the Frost and Mountain Giants were touched with kindness and came to do him honor. When the wife of Baldur saw the funeral pile prepared, she died of grief, and her body was consumed with that of her husband.

Loki's Punishment.

Ques. How did the gods revenge the death of Baldur?
Ans. They pursued Loki, who made use of his magical power to escape their wrath. He changed

himself at one time into a salmon, and hid among the stones of a brook. He was taken, however, by Thor, who caught him by the tail, and compressed it so, that all salmons ever since have had that part remarkably thin. Being restored to his natural form, Loki was bound with chains in a gloomy cavern. A serpent was suspended over his head, whose venom falls upon his face drop by drop. One comfort is allowed him; his wife Siguna sits by his side, and catches the drops as they fall, in a cup; but when she carries it away to empty it, the venom falls upon Loki, which makes him howl with horror, and twist his body so violently that the whole earth shakes.

The Elves.

Ques. Who were the **Elves**?

Ans. They were **beautiful** spirits, clothed in transparent and delicate garments. They loved the light, and were kindly disposed to mankind. The country of the Elves was called Alfheim, and was the domain of Freyr, the god of the sun, in whose light they were always sporting.

Ques. Were all the fairies equally beneficent?

Ans. No; the Night Elves, also called Gnomes, and sometimes Brownies, were at times exceedingly malicious. They were ugly, long-nosed dwarfs of a dark brown complexion, and were never seen except at night, because the sun's rays had the power of changing them into stones.

Ques. Where did these dwell?

Ans. The Gnomes dwelt in mountain caverns and the clefts of rocks. They were particularly distinguished for their knowledge of the mysterious powers of nature. They were also skillful workers in wood and metal, and were acquainted with the secret stores of gold and silver which the gods had hidden in the earth. Many stories are related of their malicious pranks; but they sometimes favored the poor and friendless in an unexpected manner.

The principal works of the Gnomes were Thor's hammer, and the ship Skidbladnir. This vessel was so wonderfully wrought, that while it was large enough to carry all the deities with their war and household implements, it could be folded together so small as to be carried in the hand.

Runic Letters.

Ques. What are Runic-letters?

Ans. One may occasionally meet in Norway Denmark, or Sweden with great stones of different forms, engraven with characters called Runic, which appear, at first sight, very different from any letters we know. They consist almost invariably of straight lines in the shape of little sticks, either single or in groups. Divination was anciently practiced among the northern nations by means of sticks of different lengths. These were shaken up, and from the chance figures they formed, the priests predicted future events.

When alphabetic writing was introduced, the letters naturally took the form of the ancient runes. The magic verses were of various kinds. The noxious, or, as they were called, the bitter runes were recited to bring evils on their enemies; the favorable averted misfortune; some were medicinal, others employed to win love, etc. In later times, the runes were used for inscriptions, of which more than a thousand have been found.

The language is a dialect of the Gothic, called Norse, still in use in Iceland. The inscriptions may, therefore, be read with certainty; but they throw very little light on history, being principally epitaphs on tombstones.

Ragnarok, the Twilight of the Gods.

It was a firm belief of the northern nations, that a time would come when all the visible creation, the gods of Valhalla, the inhabitants of earth, men, giants and elves, would be destroyed, together with their habitations.

This fearful day will not be without its forerunners. First will come a triple winter, during which clouds of snow, driven by piercing winds from the four quarters of the heavens, will fall unceasingly on the earth; tempests will sweep the sea, and the sun will impart neither heat nor gladness. Three such winters will pass away without being tempered by a single summer.

Three other winters will then follow, during which war and discord will convulse the universe. The solid earth will tremble, the sea will leave its bed, and the heavens will be rent asunder.

During this convulsion of nature, armies will meet in combat, and so great shall be the slaughter, that wolves and eagles will banquet upon the flesh of kings and heroes. The wolf Fenris will now break his bands; the Midgard serpent rise out of the sea, and Loki, released from his chains, will join the enemies of the gods. The Eddas give a wild description of the last great battlefield on which the powers of good and evil shall contend, and on which all alike, whether gods or demons, are doomed to perish. When all are slain, the world will be wrapped in flames, the sun will become dim, the stars will fall from heaven, and time shall be no more.

After this universal destruction, Alfâdur (All-Father) will cause a new heaven and a new earth to rise out of the abyss. This new earth will produce its fruits without labor or care; perpetual spring will reign, and sin and misery will be unknown. In this blissful abode, gods and men are to dwell together in a peace which the powers of evil can never again disturb.

Germany.

The Mythology of the Teutonic or Germanic race is neither so picturesque nor so well defined as that of Scandinavia. Odin and other Scandinavian divinities were worshipped by the tribes who dwelt along the borders of the Northern Ocean; in other parts of Germany, Druidism prevailed. The Germans had, however, their own deities and their own superstitions. Tuisco (sometimes written Tuesco or Tuisto) was worshipped by the Saxons as the god of war. The third day of the week takes its name from this divinity.

CHAPTER VIII.

CELTIC MYTHOLOGY

DRUIDISM.

Ques. From what is the term Druid derived?

Ans. There exists much difference of opinion on this point. The word has been variously deduced from the Saxon, "dry," a magician, from the German, "druthin," a master or lord, from the Celtic, "deru," an oak, etc. The best informed writers now refer it to the compound Celtic word "derouyd," from "De," God, and "rouyd," speaking. It would, therefore, seem to signify those who speak of or for God.

Ques. Where did Druidism prevail?

Ans. In some parts of Germany, in Gaul, and in ancient Britain and Ireland.

Ques. Where did it originate?

Ans. Various theories have been advanced on this subject. Some refer it to the Siva-worshippers of Hindostan, others to the Magi of Persia; but all agree as to its Eastern origin.

Ques. Who is the earliest writer on this subject?

Ans. Julius Cæsar. His account is considered perfectly reliable, although, to render it more intelligible, he gives to the Celtic gods the names of the Greek and Roman divinities whom they resemble.

Ques. What were the principal characteristics of Druidism?

Ans. The belief in one Supreme Being: in the immortality of the soul, and a future state of rewards and punishments. This last doctrine takes with them, as with the Hindoos, the form of metempsychosis. The religion of the Druids was farther characterized by the use of circular temples, open at the top; the worship of fire as the emblem of the sun, and the celebration of the ancient Tauric festival, (held on the first of May, when the sun enters Taurus.)

Ques. What name did the Druids give to the Supreme Being?

Ans. Esus, or Hesus; although this is sometimes mentioned as the appellation of a subordinate divinity. Superior to the Roman Jupiter, or the Zeus of the Greeks, Esus had no parentage; was subject to no fate; he was free and self-existent, and the creation of the world was his own voluntary act. The Druids taught that excepting this Supreme God, all things had a beginning, but that nothing created would ever have an end. Notwithstanding these enlightened ideas, they reverenced many other divinities. The Assyrian Baal was worshipped among the Celts as Bel or Belen. As he represented the sun, the Romans recognized in him their god Apollo. Diodorus Siculus, a contemporary of Cæsar, makes the following statement on the authority of an ancient Greek writer.

"Apollo," he says, "is worshipped with solemn rites by the inhabitants of a large island, which lies off the coast of Gaul, in the Northern Ocean. This island is inhabited by the Hyperboreans, so named because they live beyond the region of the north wind. The god has there a remarkable temple, circular in form, and a magnificent forest is consecrated to him." It is generally supposed that the temple alluded to by Diodorus, was the Druidical circle of Stonehenge, of which we shall speak later.

Ques. Who was Teu'tates?

Ans. This name is thought to be derived from "Tut-tat," signifying 'parent of men." This god was much honored by the Gauls, who attributed to him the invention of letters and poetry. According to the Triads, (Druidical verses,) he "wrote upon stone the arts and the sciences of the world." In his more beneficent character, the name Gwyon was often given to this divinity. He resembles, both in name and attributes, Thoth, the Mercury of Egypt and Phœnicia. The ancient Gauls had no idols, nor did they ever attempt any visible representation of their deities. When the Romans established their own worship in the country, they endeavored, according to their usual policy, to conciliate the conquered tribes by adopting their gods, and placing their images in the temples which they built. We read that Zenodorus, a famous sculptor, said by some to have been a native of Gaul, excuted a statue of Teu'tates which cost forty million sestertia. He spent six years upon this great work.

Camul, the Celtic Mars, Tarann, the god of thunder, and many other divinities of inferior rank, were worshipped in Gaul and Germany.

Ques. How was the Druid priesthood divided?

Ans. Into three orders; the priests, the bards, and the Druids, properly so called.

Ques. What were the duties of the priests?

Ans. They studied the hidden laws of nature and the mysteries of earth and heaven. They offered public and private sacrifices, and obtained a knowledge of the future from the entrails and the blood of victims, or from the flight of birds. They also cured maladies with certain mysterious charms. The bards held a still higher rank: they preserved in their verses the mystic learning of the priests, the traditions of their race, and the great actions of their heroes. No sacrifice was duly offered without their sacred chant; they encouraged the warrior going to the field of combat, and received him on his return with notes of triumph. To live in heroic song was the aspiration of every Celtic warrior, and to the coward or traitor, there was no penalty so terrible as the denunciation of the sacred bards. Music was the only gentle art known to the rude tribes of Gaul and Britain, and they were, perhaps for this reason, the more susceptible to its influence. The character of these minstrels was peculiarly sacred in their eyes, on account of the gifts of prophecy and second sight which they were believed to possess in moments of inspiration.

The verses of the bards were never committed to writing, and a long and painful course of oral instruction was necessary before a candidate could be admitted to take his place in this influential class. According to Cæsar, twenty years was the ordinary novitiate required.

The bards of Gaul seem to have passed away with the religious system to which they belonged; but in the British islands, they continued, although divested of their sacred character, to be a highly esteemed and privileged class. We may judge of their influence in keeping alive the patriotic spirit of the people, from the fact that Edward I. ordered their extermination as the surest means of extinguishing the feeling of nationality among the Welsh tribes. In Ireland and Scotland, the bards gradually passed away with the decline of the feudal system, and the power of the native princes and chieftains whose glory they sung.

Ques. Who were the Druids, properly so called?

Ans. They were priests of the highest order, who remained secluded in caves and grottoes, or in the depths of oak forests, where they were sup posed to study the deeper mysteries of nature and religion, and to consult more directly the secret will of the divinity. They were also the teachers of youth.

The Druids must have possessed some knowledge of the motions of the heavenly bodies, since they counted the year by lunations; astronomical instruments have also been found among the druidical remains in Ireland, which prove that they had made a certain progress in this science. Like the Persians, they mingled astrology and divination with their observations of the celestial bodies. The healing art was also practised by the Druids. The effect of their remedies was not, however, attributed to any natural cause, but rather to a mysterious virtue residing in certain plants, and rendered efficacious by the magic rites with which they were gathered.

The mistletoe, when found growing on the oak, was esteemed particularly sacred; it was an antidote against poison, a remedy in all diseases, and a preservative against the machinations of evil spirits. To possess the proper efficacy, it should be gathered in February or March, on the sixth day of the moon. As soon as the mistletoe was found growing on the no less sacred oak, the Druids assembled; a banquet and a sacrifice were prepared, after which a priest in white vestments cut the plant with a golden sickle while two others received it reverently into a white mantle spread beneath. Two milk-white heifers were instantly offered in sacrifice, and the rest of the day was spent in rejoicing. In like manner, the samolus, or marsh-wort, possessed no virtue unless it were sought fasting, and gathered with the left hand, without looking at it. They plucked the helago, or hedge hyssop, barefooted, and without a knife, after ablutions, and offerings of bread and wine. The vervain and other plants had also their distinct ceremonial.

Amber was valued for certain mysterious properties; it was manufactured into beads by the Druids, and these were given as charms to warriors going to battle; such beads are sometimes found in their tombs.

Ques. Were the Druids acquainted with the art of writing?

Ans. They were, at least in Gaul and Ireland. Their alphabet contained seventeen letters, and resembled the characters used by the ancient Pelasgi. It is probable, therefore, that they received it from the early Greek colonists. Writing was employed for ordinary affairs, whether public or private, but the mystic learning of the Druids was handed down by oral tradition only. The few inscriptions they have left are in symbolic writing, which resembles the runes of Scandinavia, and originated in the same manner from the rods and branches of certain plants used in divination. These inscriptions are called in Ireland "ogham;" they are principally straight lines, grouped in different ways.

Ques. Did the Druids exercise any political authority?

Ans. Yes; they were the legislators of the people, and had the right of deciding in all controversies. There was no appeal from their sentence, and those who ventured to resist were excommunicated and outlawed.

The college of Druids was governed by a chief or Arch-druid, chosen by vote from among their number. The elections were eagerly contested, and were often attended with much bloodshed. The Arch-druid held his office for life.

Ques. Who were the Druidesses?

Ans. They were prophetesses or sorceresses, most generally wives or daughters of the Druids, who exercised an unbounded influence over the people. They were supposed to read the future, to conjure tempests, and appease them again at will. The Gallic mariner often went to consult them amid the reefs of the Armorican coast, and trembled with superstitious awe as he saw them gliding like phantoms among the misty crags, waving flaming torches, and mingling their wild chants with the voices of wind and sea. Some of these sorceresses were obliged to assist at nocturnal rites, where, with their bodies painted black, and their hair dishevelled, they joined in a frantic dance, and abandoned themselves to the wildest transports of frenzy. A peculiar rite was practised by the Druidesses who resided in an island at the mouth of the Loire. They were obliged once every year, between sunrise and sunset, to demolish and rebuild the roof of their rustic temple. If any of their number should let fall the least part of the sacred material, her fate was sealed. She was torn to pieces by her companions, amid paroxysms of wild frenzy which recalled to the Greeks the orgies of their own Bacchantes. It is said that no year passed without a victim.

The nine virgin priestesses who dwelt on the island of Sena, an almost inaccessible rock off the promontory of Plogoff, on the coast of Brittany, were regarded with particular veneration, and constituted, perhaps, the highest religious authority among the ancient Gauls. There was a class of Druidesses in Gaul and Germany, who, in addition to practices of sorcery and incantation, presided at fearful rites. Strabo tells us that when the Cimbri had taken prisoners of war, they were offered in sacrifice by these terrible women. The chief Druidess, standing by a rude stone altar, received the victim dragged thither by her companions. She plunged her knife into his heart, and watched carefully to obtain an omen, according as the blood should flow more or less rapidly. This ceremony was repeated with other victims until the augury was deemed decisive. The superstitions with regard to witches and their nocturnal revels, which prevailed so long in Europe, originated, no doubt, from popular traditions concerning these sorceresses.

In Ireland, they do not appear to have played either so terrible or so important a part. We only know that at Tara, certain virgins of royal blood were consecrated to Baal and Samhain, (the moon,) and watched the perpetual fire which burned on their altars. In one of the civil wars so common in the island, a chief of Leinster destroyed this sanctuary and massacred its inmates. The entire country united to punish the perpetrators of this sacrilege; they were put to death, and a perpetual fine was imposed on the province of Leinster.

Ques. What sacrifices were offered by the Druids?

Ans. In time of peace, fruits and cattle; in war, human sacrifices were preferred.

Ques. How were the victims chosen?

Ans. They were generally captives taken in war, slaves or criminals. In some cases, warriors and others devoted themselves voluntarily to the altar, either to propitiate the gods, and obtain victory for their people, or because they were weary of life, and desired to hasten the moment of transmigration. These acts of self-immolation were esteemed exceedingly meritorious. Cæsar supposes Teu'tates to be the same with Dis or Pluto; but in the mythology of the Gauls, there were no infernal regions, and consequently, there was no Pluto The soul passed into another body, and the transmigration was happy, or the contrary, as the actions performed during its last state of existence had been good or evil.

According to the Druids, death was but the central point of a long life.

Ques. What was the usual mode of sacrifice?

Ans. Victims offered to Baal were always burned. On important occasions, a great number were enclosed in a huge frame of wicker work in which they were consumed together. In offerings to other gods, different rites were observed.

These remarks apply chiefly to Gaul, Germany and Britain. Human sacrifices were rare in Ireland.

Ques. What were the principal festivals of the Druids?

Ans. The Tauric festival, which has been already mentioned, was the most ancient, dating from the time of the Chaldees, or Babylonians. In Ireland and in the Highlands of Scotland, the first of May takes its name from this solemnity, being called in Gaelic, Beltane; and in Irish, Beal-Tinne, or the Fire of Baal. The solstices were also celebrated as the chief points in the sun's annual course. Wherever Druidism prevailed, there was in the centre of each great district or canton, a perpetual fire in honor of Baal. On the feast of the god, this was extinguished, and again lighted, after which all the fires throughout the country were rekindled from this sacred source. This rite was observed with particular solemnity in Ireland. There the Druids assembled around the sacred or "parent fire," which the Arch-druid extinguished. At this signal every fire disappeared, and, in an incredibly short space of time, darkness settled on the island. The chiefs and princes, together with the assembled people, then assisted in silent awe, while the Druids performed their nocturnal rites. At length the fire was rekindled; torches lighted at the sacred flame were passed from hand to hand, and the country was soon illuminated by the Baal fires which blazed on every hill. The chief scene of these solemnities was Ouisneach, in the centre of the island, but the same rite was performed in many other places.

According to what seems an authentic tradition, it was during such a ceremony that St. Patrick obtained the opportunity of holding a public disputation with the Druids in the presence of the king and chieftains assembled at Tara. It was Easter Eve, and the Saint, who must have been well aware of the penalty of death attached to such an act, commanded his disciples to light the paschal fire at the moment when all around was plunged in darkness. The flame was seen at Tara, and the Druids called loudly for the punishment of the sacrilegious strangers. They were seized and brought before the assembly, but the result was favorable to the missionaries, and from that day may be dated the rapid though peaceful decline of Druidism in Ireland.

The idolatrous rites peculiar to the season of

the summer solstice have been long forgotten but the custom of lighting fires upon that day, still prevails. The bonfires of St. John's Eve (June 21st) recall, at least, one feature of the ancient Druid festival.

Ques. What rites were observed on the first day of November?

Ans. The day was consecrated to the Moon, (called in Ireland Samhain,) and was observed both in Gaul and in the British islands. It would seem that the spirits of the departed were also propitiated at this season, and many curious traditions are connected with its observance.

Before the invasion of Cæsar, Britain was so little known to the ancient Gauls, as to be still a land of mystery. They believed that on every feast of the moon, the souls of those who had died during the year, were obliged to repair thither for judgment.

Connected with this, Procopius relates an Armorican legend of which some traces may yet be found in Brittany. At the foot of the promontory of Plogoff, around the sacred isle of Sena, are scattered rocks on which the sea breaks with an unceasing moan. Thither assemble, on the night of judgment, the spirits of the dead. Faint wailings are heard, and pale phantoms are seen gliding above the waves, which they are not yet spiritual enough to cross without human succor. At the hour of midnight the sailors and fisher men along the coast hear mysterious voices calling at their doors. They rise and find strange barks waiting on the shore. Scarcely have they entered these, when the light craft is weighed down by a ghostly band. The terrified pilot has no need of helm or sail, for the barks are borne westwardly with incredible velocity. When they touch the misty shores of Britain, there is a hollow murmur—the boats ride lightly on the water —the souls are gone.

The superstitious observances which are still practised on November, or All Hallow Eve, in Ireland, Scotland, and some parts of England, are of pagan origin, and seem to be relics of this festival.

Ques. At what period may we fix the decline of Druidism?

Ans. It was suppressed in Gaul by the Roman conquerors, who built temples, and introduced the worship of their own gods, adopting also those of the conquered race. Druidism retired, step by step, before this more classic heathenism, but found a temporary refuge in the German forests and in Armorica. It was suppressed in Britain during the reign of Nero. The persecuted Druids took refuge in the island of Mona or Anglesea, whence they were driven by the Roman troops with great slaughter. They found a last asylum in the island of Iona. Here they maintained a certain influence up to the latter part of the sixth century, when the inhabitants of the island were converted by the preaching of St

Columba, the Apostle of the Highlands. This missionary was a native of Ireland, where Christianity had been established for nearly a century.

Ques. What traces still remain of the ancient Druidical worship?

Ans. Certain monuments, which are called, according to their form, menhirs, dolmens or cromlechs.

Ques. What are the menhirs?

Ans. The word is derived from the old Breton man, stone; and hir, long. They are upright blocks of stone, often terminating in a point; and are for the most part rough and unshapely; the ordinary height is from seven to twelve feet; but in some rare instances, they exceed thirty feet in height. The purpose of these menhirs is not well understood. Where they stand singly, or in groups of two or three, they probably mark a spot rendered memorable by some important event. Similar monuments were common in primitive times, as we learn from Scripture; when the Israelites had crossed the dry bed of the Jordan, Joshua placed twelve stones on the bank, as a remembrance of the miracle. Jacob marked in the same manner the spot on which he had been favored by a celestial vision. In certain places on the Scandinavian peninsula, extensive groups ef menhirs occur, scattered irregularly over the plain; these are supposed to mark ancient battle-fields. Where the stones are arranged in a " cromlech " or circular form, there is generally a dolmen in the centre. The dolmen is a large flat stone, placed like a table, upon two others which are set upright. Some of these were evidently altars, as the flat stone on the top is furrowed and slightly inclined to facilitate as it were the flowing of blood. Dolmens are found also in straight lines, forming a sort of covered gallery.

Ques. Where are the most remarkable of these monuments?

Ans. On the continent of Europe, the most extensive series is that of Carnac in Brittany. In the midst of a wide heath, stand rude blocks of gray granite, set on end; they are angular, and show no marks of polish. These menhirs are arranged in eleven lines, forming regular alleys The blocks numbered formerly about ten thousand; but there are now many gaps in the stony lines, as every house in the vicinity seems to have been built from this convenient quarry.

At Stonehenge, in England, is a large cromlech arranged in two circles and two ovals. There are in all about one hundred and forty stones, of which the smallest are estimated to weigh ten or twelve, and the largest seventy tons. In the centre of the work is a massive slab of fine sandstone, supposed to have been an altar. This cromlech is surrounded by a trench and an earthen embankment. Numerous ancient *barrows*, or burial mounds, are found in the neighborhood. In Ireland, monuments constructed of stone are sometimes found; but circular earthworks are more common. In this country, as in Brittany, many popular superstitions still attach to these remains of ancient paganism. Almost within our own day, many an Irish peasant has made his scanty harvest still smaller, rather than violate with the plough, the grass-grown "rath," or Druid circle. Death within the year is the supposed penalty of such an act. In Brittany, malignant dwarfs and night-elves still haunt the deserted cromlech, and have power at certain times, to wreak their malice on the belated traveller. Some of these giant stones are themselves subject to mysterious laws. Once in a hundred years, they are obliged, at the hour of midnight, to pass in weird procession to bathe in the waters of the Northern Ocean.

Then for a few brief moments the stars look down on the riches buried in ancient times beneath the enchanted circle. It is the treasure-seeker's golden opportunity, but woe to the avaricious wretch who lingers over the spoil. He is crushed by the swift returning stones, and the morning sun finds the grim sentinels silent and motionless as before, bearing no trace of their wild nocturnal march.

CHAPTER IX.

Mexico.

MYTHOLOGY OF THE AZTECS

Ques. What peculiarity has been remarked in the mythology of the Aztecs or ancient Mexicans?

Ans. Its incongruity. On the one hand we find their priests inculcating the most sublime truths of natural religion, and the purest maxims of morality, while on the other, their sacrifices and public worship were marked by a spirit of unexampled ferocity.

Ques. How has this been explained?

Ans. It is supposed that the religion of the Aztecs was derived from two distinct sources. The ancient Toltecs, who preceded them in Mexico, were a comparatively humane and enlightened race; they retained many of the highest principles of natural religion, united, probably, with truths derived from primitive tradition. The Aztecs seem to have adopted the religion of their more civilized predecessors without abandoning their own dark and cruel superstitions. Hence the contradictions and inconsistencies of their mythology.

Ques. What did the Aztecs believe of God?

Ans. They believed in one Supreme Lord and Creator, to whom they attributed all the divine perfections. The prayers which they addressed to Him recall, in many instances, the very phraseology of Scripture.

Ques. Did the Aztecs worship any other deity?

Ans. Yes, they worshipped many subordinate divinities who were supposed to preside over the elements, the changes of the seasons and the various occupations of men. Of these gods, thirteen held the most exalted rank, while the inferior class numbered over two hundred.

Ques. Who may be considered the chief of these subordinate divinities?

Ans. Huitzilopotchli, a sort of Mexican Mars, who was, in fact, the patron deity of the nation. His temples were the most stately of all the public edifices, and his altars in every part of the empire were continually reeking with the blood of human victims.

Ques. Who was Quetzalcoatl?

Ans. The Aztecs, like many nations of the old world, had their Golden Age. During this blissful period, Quetzalcoatl, god of the air, dwelt on earth, and instructed men in the use of metals, in agriculture and every useful art. Under his beneficent rule, the earth brought forth its fruits without care or labor: and such was the fertility of the soil that a single ear of corn was as much as a man could carry. The dyer's art was not needed, for the cotton took, as it grew, the richest and most varied hues. The rarest flowers filled the air with perfume, and the melody of birds was heard in every grove. This happy state was not destined to last; Quetzalcoatl incurred the anger of one of the greater gods, and was obliged to abandon the country. He proceeded to the shores of the Mexican gulf, where he took leave of his followers, promising that, when many years had rolled away, he would revisit their descendants. He then embarked in a skiff made of serpent's skins, and sailed eastward towards the fabled land of Tlapallan.

Quetzalcoatl was described by the Mexicans as tall, with a fair complexion, long, dark hair, and a flowing beard. They looked confidently for the return of the benevolent deity, and this tradition had no small influence in preparing the way for the future success of the Spaniards.

It is evident that Quetzalcoatl was the name given by the Mexicans to some beneficent ruler who instructed them in the arts of civilized life. It is singular that he should have been described with every characteristic of the European race; and some have conjectured that he was indeed a native of the Eastern hemisphere, cast by some strange accident among the simple natives of the New World.

MYTHOLOGY OF THE AZTECS. 277

Ques. Did the Aztecs worship any household divinities?

Ans. Yes; the images of their penates, or household gods, were to be found in every dwelling.

Ques. What did the Aztecs believe with regard to a future life?

Ans. Their priests taught that the wicked were sent after death to expiate their sins in a region of eternal darkness. Those who died of certain diseases were entitled, after death, to a state of indolent contentment; but the Aztec paradise, like the Elysium of the Greeks and Romans, was reserved for their warriors and heroes. In this class were included those who were offered in sacrifice. These privileged souls passed at once into the presence of the Sun, whom they accompanied with songs and choral dances in his journey through the heavens. After a certain period, their spirits went to animate the golden clouds which floated over the gardens of paradise, or, assuming the form of singing birds, revelled amid the blossoms and odors of its sacred groves.

Ques. What peculiar rite was practised by the Aztecs in the naming of their children?

Ans. The lips and bosom of the infant were sprinkled with water. During the ceremony they implored the Lord, that the holy drops might wash away the sin that was given to it before the foundation of the world, so that the child might be born anew.

Ques. How did the Aztecs bury their dead?

Ans. Immediately after death, the corpse was clothed in certain sacred habiliments, and strewed with charms, which were supposed to be necessary as a defence against the dangers of the unknown road which the spirit was about to travel. The body was then burned, and the ashes, carefully collected in a funeral urn, were placed in the house of the deceased. In this mode of burial, we may notice a certain resemblance to the funeral rites of the ancient Greeks and Romans. There was, however, this distinction, that although the latter occasionally sacrificed their captive enemies to the manes of a departed warrior, this offering formed no necessary part of the burial rite; on the other hand, the obsequies of an Aztec noble were always accompanied by the sacrifice of unoffending slaves, the number of victims being proportioned to the rank of the deceased.

Ques. Did the Aztec priests form a distinct order?

Ans. They were altogether distinct from the people, and formed a numerous and powerful hierarchy. Their different functions were exactly regulated; those who were best skilled in music formed the choirs—Others arranged the festivals according to the calendar. Some were engaged in the education of youth, and others had charge of the hieroglyphical paintings and oral traditions, while the dreadful rites of sacrifice were reserved to the chief dignitaries of the order.

Ques. Were women permitted to exercise any sacerdotal functions?

Ans. Yes; the Aztec priestesses exercised every function except that of sacrifice. They superintended the schools in which the daughters of the higher and middle classes received their education. These schools, as well as those for boys, directed by the priests, were under the strictest discipline. Ordinary faults were punished with extreme rigor; graver offences, with death.

Ques. How was this numerous priesthood maintained?

Ans. A certain quantity of land was annexed to each temple, and the priests were further enriched by first fruits and other offerings. This large provision became necessary from the fact that the Aztec priests were allowed to marry. The law prescribed that any surplus, beyond what was actually required for their support, should be distributed among the poor. This, and other benevolent provisions, seem very inconsistent with the cruelties practised in their public worship.

Ques. What was the form of the Mexican temples?

Ans. They were solid pyramids, constructed of earth, but completely cased in brick or stone. They were disposed in three or four stories, each smaller than that below. At the top was a broad area, in which stood one or more towers, containing images of the presiding deities. Before these towers were generally placed, besides the dreadful stone of sacrifice, two lofty altars on which burned perpetual fires. So numerous were these sacred fires in the city of Mexico, that the streets were brilliantly lighted even on the darkest night. The ascent was made, in some cases, by a stairway which led directly up the centre of the western face of the pyramid. More generally, it was so arranged, that the religious processions were obliged to pass two or three times around the pyramid before reaching the summit. The Mexicans called their temples Teocallis, or "houses of God."

Ques. Are any of these structures still in existence?

Ans. Yes; of those which yet remain, the pyramid of Cholula is the largest, and perhaps the most perfect. It mearsures 176 feet in perpendicular height, and is 1425 feet square; it covers 45 acres. It is very ancient, having been built before the Aztecs conquered Anahuac, as that part of Mexico was formerly named.

Ques. What sacrifices were offered by the Aztecs?

Ans. Their sacrifices present the same striking contrasts which we find in everything connected with their religion.—Some festivals were of a light and joyous character, being celebrated with choral songs and dances. Processions of votaries crowned with garlands, bore offerings to the temple; fruits, ripe maize, and the sweet incense of the copal and other odoriferous gums; while the birds and domestic animals offered in sacrifice were consumed at the banquets with which the festival concluded. These innocent rites were evidently of Toltec origin; the dreadful practice of human sacrifice was introduced by the Aztec conquerors, whose wars were often undertaken for no other purpose than to procure victims for their altars.

Ques. Were these sacrifices numerous?

Ans. They were introduced only about two hundred years before the Spanish Conquest. They were at first exceptional, but became more frequent as the Aztec empire extended, until the number of those sacrificed annually throughout the empire is calculated at twenty thousand, which is the lowest estimate given. It was customary to preserve the skulls of the victims in buildings erected for the purpose. One hundred and thirty-six thousand of these ghastly relics were counted in a single edifice. Women were occasionally offered in sacrifice, but Tlaloc, the god of rain, could only be propitiated by the blood of young children and infants. In seasons of drought, these innocent victims, decked in the richest attire, and crowned with flowers, were borne to the temple in open litters, their cries being drowned in the wild chanting of the priests.

The feast of Tezcatlipoca, one of the chief gods, who was called the "Soul of the World," was celebrated by the sacrifice of a single victim, with regard to whom many peculiar ceremonies were observed. A year before the sacrifice, a young man, distinguished for grace and beauty, was chosen from among the captives. He was splendidly attired, surrounded by every luxury, and was received everywhere with the homage due to the divinity whom he was supposed to represent.

When the fatal day arrived, the victim, who had been trained to perform his part with calmness and dignity, was conducted to the temple. As the melancholy procession wound up the sides of the pyramid, he played upon a musical instrument; at first, joyous airs, which grew graver and more mournful as the cortege advanced, until at length he broke his lute, and cast it aside. He then threw from him, one by one, his chaplets of flowers, and stood unadorned before the stone of sacrifice. The bloody work was soon accomplished, and the yet palpitating heart of the victim was thrown at the feet of the idol. The career of this captive, and his progress to the altar, was intended as an allegorical representation of human life, which, joyous at first, terminates in sorrow and in death. In speaking of human sacrifices, we have yet to mention the most revolting feature. The Mexicans, both men and women, feasted on the bodies of the victims; and no Aztec noble would venture to entertain his friends on a festival day without placing before them this loathsome food.

It is worthy of remark that Montezuma surpassed all his predecessors in the pomp with which he celebrated the festivals of the Aztec gods, and the number of human victims which he offered on their altars.

CHAPTER X.

PERU.

Ques. What deities were worshipped by the ancient Peruvians?

Ans. Like most of the races inhabiting the American continent, the Peruvians believed in one Supreme God, immaterial and infinite. This sublime doctrine did not, however, lead to the practical results that might have been expected.

Ques. What name did the Peruvians give to this Supreme deity?

Ans. He was adored under the different names of Pachacamac and Viracocha. They raised no temples in his honor; that which stood near the present site of Lima, having been erected before the country came under the sway of the Incas. It seems probable, therefore, that the worship of this Great Spirit did not originate with the Peruvians. Their entire system of religion was directed to the adoration of the heavenly bodies. The Sun was adored as the father of the world, the source of light and life. The Moon was honored as his sister-wife, and the

Stars were worshipped as her heavenly train. The planet known to us as Venus was an especial object of devotion. The Peruvians named it Chasca, or "the Youth with the long and curling locks;" they worshipped it as the page of the Sun, whom he attends in his rising and setting.

The Sun was honored also as the father of the royal Inca race; and, connected with this belief, we have one of the few legends worthy of note in the barren mythology of the Peruvians.

Ques. Relate this legend.

Ans. According to tradition, there was a time when the ancient races of the continent were plunged in the most complete barbarism: the will of the strongest was the only law; war was their pastime; they worshipped the vilest objects in nature, and feasted on the flesh of their slaughtered enemies. The Sun, the great parent of mankind, took compassion on their degraded state, and sent two of his children, Manco-Capac, and Mama Oello Huaco, to form men into regular communities, and teach them the arts of civilized life. The celestial pair advanced along the high plains in the neighborhood of Lake Titicaca, as far as the sixteenth degree of south latitude. They bore with them a golden wedge, and were directed to take up their abode wherever the sacred emblem should sink into the earth of its own accord. This prodigy took place in the valley of Cuzco, where the wedge sank into the ground, and disappeared forever. Here the children of the Sun entered upon their benevolent mission; Manco-Capac instructing the men in the arts of agriculture, while Mama Oello initiated the women into the mysteries of weaving and spinning. The rude, but simple-hearted natives were not slow to appreciate the benefits conferred by the messengers of heaven: a large community was gradually formed, and the city of Cuzco was founded in the valley. The monarchy thus formed, was governed by the Incas, who claimed descent from Manco-Capac and Mama Oello, and always styled themselves, Children of the Sun.

Ques. What was the origin of this legend?

Ans. It was evidently a fiction, invented at a later period to gratify the vanity of the Incas, by attributing to their race a celestial origin. The extensive ruins on the shores of Lake Titicaca prove that this region was inhabited by a powerful, and comparatively civilized people, long before the foundation of the Peruvian monarchy.

Ques. Are there any other Peruvian legends?

Ans. Among the traditions of this race, is one of the deluge, which resembles in one or two curious particulars the Mexican legend on the same subject. According to both these traditions, seven persons took refuge in caves, in which they were preserved from the universal destruction; and from these, the earth was re-peopled. The Peruvians maintained that white and bearded men from the east had visited the country in ancient times, and instructed the natives in the arts of civilized life. This legend recalls the Mexican story of Quetzalcoatl, and the coincidence is singular, because no communication is believed to have existed between the two countries.

Ques. Where were the most celebrated temples of the Sun?

Ans. The most ancient of these edifices was in the island of Titicaca, whence the founders of the Inca dynasty were said to have proceeded. Everything belonging to this sanctuary was held in particular veneration. Even the fields of maize which were attached to the temple were supposed to partake of its sanctity; and the yearly produce was distributed in small quantities through all the public granaries, to bring a blessing on the rest of the store.

A Peruvian esteemed himself happy in securing even a single ear of the sacred grain.

Ques. Describe the temple of Cuzco.

Ans. This edifice was constructed of stone, and covered a large extent of ground in the heart of the city. The interior of the temple has been described, by those who saw it in its glory, as being literally a mine of precious metals. It was called by the natives Coricancha, or "Place of Gold." On the western wall was the image of the Sun; this was a massive golden plate, of enormous dimensions, on which was emblazoned a human countenance darting forth rays on every side, The image was richly ornamented with emeralds and precious stones. It fronted the eastern portal of the temple in such a manner that the first rays of the morning Sun fell directly on his golden image, and were reflected from the rich ornaments with which the walls and ceiling were encrusted. Every part of the temple glowed with the precious metal, and even the exterior was encompassed with a broad frieze of gold set in the solid stone-work of the edifice. Adjoining the principal structure was the temple of the Moon. Her effigy was of silver, but otherwise resembled that of the Sun. The same metal was used in all the decorations of the building, as resembling in its pale lustre the milder radiance of the beautiful planet.

One chapel was dedicated to the stars, another to thunder and lightning, and a third to the rainbow. This last was decorated with a many-colored arch of resplendent hues. Attached to the temple of Cuzco were the celebrated gardens, sparkling with flowers of gold and silver. Animals also were represented in precious ore, and the classic fable of the golden fleece was realized in the llama of this fairy garden.

Ques. Does anything now remain of this magnificent temple?

Ans. No; its riches became the prey of the conquerors, and the desecrated shrine offered an inexhaustible supply of material for the erection of other buildings. Fields of maize are now waving where the golden gardens once sparkled in the sun, and the church of St. Dominic, one of the most magnificent buildings of the New World, occupies the site of the famous Coricancha. The temples of Peru were many and magnificent; but Cuzco was to the Inca noble what Mecca is to the devout follower of Mahomet, and he would consider that he had neglected a sacred duty, if he had not made at least one pilgrimage to the holy shrine.

Ques. From what class were the Peruvian priests generally chosen?

Ans. They were all, without exception, Inca nobles, and therefore children of the Sun. The High Priest, called Villac Vmu, was second only to the Inca, and was chosen from among his brothers or nearest kindred.

Ques. What sacrifices were offered to the Sun?

Ans. Animals, ripe maize, flowers and sweet-scented gums. Human sacrifices were rare, and were only offered on great occasions, such as a coronation, a victory, etc. A child or a beautiful maiden was then selected as the victim; but the cannibal repasts of the Mexicans were unknown among the more refined Peruvians.

Ques. What were the principal festivals of the Sun?

Ans. The solstices and equinoxes were celebrated by four great festivals; but the most solemn was the feast of Raymi, held at the period of their summer solstice. This festival lasted many days. The animals offered in sacrifice were served at the tables of the Inca and of his nobles; but of the flocks belonging to the temple, a vast number were slaughtered and distributed among the people.

Ques. What points of resemblance have been noticed between the religious observances of the Peruvians and those of the ancient Romans?

Ans. In the mode of procuring the sacred fire, the obtaining of omens from the animals offered in sacrifice, and in some of the laws with regard to the Virgins of the Sun. At the festival of Raymi, the sacred fire was obtained, as under the reign of Numa, by means of a concave mirror of polished metal. The sun's rays were in this manner collected in a focus of sufficient intensity to ignite dried cotton. When the sky was overcast, which was esteemed a very bad omen, the fire was obtained by means of friction. This fire was watched by the Virgins of the Sun.

Ques. Who were these?

Ans. They were maidens of noble birth who were dedicated to the service of the Sun. They were taken from their families at an early age, and placed under the care of elderly matrons, who instructed them in their religious duties, and in every branch of female industry. They spun garments, which they were taught to embroider with exquisite skill. They also wove, of the fine hair of the vicuña, the hangings of the temples and the garments worn by the Inca and his household. They were completely secluded, even from their own nearest relatives. The wives of the Inca, and they were numerous, were chosen from among the Virgins of the Sun. With this exception, they were forbidden to marry. The unhappy maiden who ventured to form in secret a less exalted alliance, was condemned to the cruel punishment decreed in like circumstances against the Roman Vestal. She was buried alive; her accomplice was strangled, and the village to which he belonged was razed to the ground and sowed with stones.

Ques. How did the Peruvians bury their dead?

Ans. The body was embalmed, not, as in Egypt, with gums and spices, but by simple exposure to the cold, dry and rarefied atmosphere of the mountains. The mummies are generally in a sitting posture. As the Peruvians imagined that the wants and occupations of men would be the same beyond the grave as in this life, costly apparel, arms, utensils and sometimes treasures were placed in the tomb of a deceased noble. That he might not lack attendance and society, his favorite wives and domestics were sacrificed on his tomb.

The Peruvians believed in an evil spirit whom they called Cupay, but they did not attempt to propitiate him by any form of worship. Cupay seems, in fact, to have been only a personification of sin.

SUPPLEMENT.

A BRIEF NOTICE OF AUTHORS, ETC., MENTIONED IN THIS VOLUME.

ÆSCHYLUS,

The earliest of the Greek dramatists, was born at Eleusis in Attica, 525 B. C. He distinguished himself in the battles of Marathon, Salamis and Platæa. Æschylus has been called the father of Grecian tragedy, as he was the first to give rules to the dialogue, and define the duties of the chorus; he also planned the dress of the actors, the scenery and the whole mechanism of the stage. Æschylus wrote sixty-six dramas, in thirteen of which he obtained the victory over all his competitors. He was at length defeated by a younger rival, Sophocles. He retired the same year to the court of Hiero, king of Syracuse, and some writers attribute this step to the mortification felt by the poet on this occasion. Others say that he was accused as guilty of profanity in exhibiting on the stage certain things connected with the Eleusinian mysteries. The people were about to stone him, when he was saved by the presence of mind of his brother Aminias. The latter had won much glory in the Persian war, and now, while interceding for his brother he dexterously dropped his mantle so as to expose the stump of the arm he had lost at Salamis. The silent appeal was not without its effect on the impulsive Athenians, and Æschylus was pardoned. He deemed it prudent, however, to retire to Sicily, where he was kindly entertained by Hiero. His death is said to have occurred in a very extraordinary manner.

As he slept in the fields, an eagle which was flying over him with a tortoise in his claws, mistook the bald head of the poet for a stone. The bird dropped the tortoise for the purpose of breaking the shell, and he was killed by the blow, thus verifying a prophecy that his death would come from on high.

Of the dramas written by Æschylus, but seven remain. Of these, the most admired is the "Prometheus Chained." The subject is the punishment of Prometheus on Mount Caucasus; the scenery is grand and terrific, and all the persons of the drama are divinities.

CÆSAR (Caius Julius),

The Roman general and dictator, holds a high rank among Latin authors. During the most active period of his life, he found time to devote to literary pursuits. Of the works written by him on various subjects, both in prose and verse, we have only his "Commentaries," in ten books. Seven of these treat of the Gallic war the rest contain an account of the Civil war. The hurry of military expeditions did not prevent this extraordinary man from observing closely the manners and customs of the different nations with whom he contended. We are indebted to the Commentaries for almost all the accurate information we possess with regard to the inhabitants of ancient Gaul.

Cæsar was not surpassed, even by the writers of the Augustan age, in clearness and beauty of style. He exaggerates nothing, and his most brilliant achievements are related with a certain modest simplicity which is one of the characteristics of true greatness.

CICERO.

A Roman orator and statesman. He filled the highest offices in the gift of his country, and took so prominent a part in public affairs, that an account of his life would be also a history of his times. Cicero wrote on the art of public speaking, on philosophy and jurisprudence. This great man, who had saved Rome from the plots of Catiline, and rendered many other signal services to his country, was basely murdered by the order of the second Triumvirate, in the year 43 B. C.

DEMOSTHENES.

A famous Athenian orator, who defended the liberties of his country against the aggressions of Philip of Macedon.

DIODORUS,

Surnamed Siculus, from Sicily, his birthplace. He was a celebrated historian, contemporary with Julius Cæsar and Augustus. He wrote a "General History" in forty books, of which we have now fifteen entire, with scattered fragments of the others. Diodorus devoted thirty years to this great work.

EURIPIDES,

A Greek tragedian, was born in 480 B. C., on the day rendered famous by the victory of Salamis. After gaining a high reputation as a dramatist, Euripides retired to Macedon, to the court of King Archelaûs. On the death of the poet, the Athenians begged that his body might be sent to Athens for interment. This request Archelaûs refused, and Euripides was buried with much pomp at Pella, in Macedon. This poet is inferior to Æschylus and Sophocles, not only in dignity of sentiment, but in the moral tone of his dramas. Sophocles is said to have observed that while he represented men as they ought to be, Euripides described them as they were.

HERODOTUS

Who has been called the Father of History, was born at Halicarnassus, 484 B. C. He spent many years travelling through Europe, Asia and Africa, observing everywhere the manners and customs of the people, and collecting materials for his great work. His account of the Persian war is full of interest, and won for him great popularity among his countrymen.

Herodotus relates many things which seem strange, and even incredible; but these are either traditions of remote times, or accounts received from other travellers. The general opinion is that where Herodotus speaks from his own observation, or relates events of which the memory was still recent, he may be relied upon as an accurate and truthful historian.

JUSTIN (Saint).

A Christian writer of the second century. He is principally celebrated for his "Apology for the Christians," addressed to the Emperor Antoninus. It is written in a style at once eloquent and persuasive, and it is believed that it had the desired effect, and was the immediate cause of the edict issued by Antoninus in favor of the Christians.

St. Justin addressed a second Apology to Marcus Aurelius, but with far different success. This Emperor was too much under the influence of the heathen philosophers whom he had assembled at his court, to judge impartially in the matter. One of these, Crescentius, a bitter enemy of the Christians, procured the death of their intrepid defender. The martyrdom of St. Justin took place at Rome, about the year 161 A. D.

JUVENAL

A Roman poet of the first century. He was born in the reign of Caligula, but the exact date is not known. Juvenal is celebrated for his satires, in which he attacked the vices and follies of his day, not sparing the emperors themselves where their conduct was deserving of reproach. Hadrian believed that one of the satires of Juvenal was directed against himself; he had not the magnanimity to overlook the offence, and Juvenal was exiled to Lybia, where he died soon after.

MÆCENAS.

Minister and favorite of the Emperor Augustus. He was distinguished for the wisdom of his counsels, and his rare abilities as a statesman. Although himself an indifferent poet, he was still a patron of literature and literary men; Virgil, Horace, Ovid and other celebrated writers of the Augustan age, were among his most intimate friends. Such was the care with which Mæcenas sought out and rewarded every species of merit, that his name is proverbially used to denote a generous patron.

Admirable in his public capacity, he was in private life as indolent and luxurious as the most effeminate oriental. His villas were laid out with unexampled magnificence, and his banquets surpassed, in taste and display, those given by Augustus himself.

The later years of Mæcenas offer a sad commentary on the value of human greatness. His constitution, which had never been strong, was weakened by excess. He was tormented by constant wakefulness, and this great man, with the resources of the world at his command, would probably have sacrificed both wealth and power for the common boon of sleep enjoyed by the meanest of his slaves. In vain the physicians exercised their skill; narcotics, monotonous sounds, distant music, all failed to produce the desired effect. A stream was, at length, conducted through a garden adjoining the chamber where he lay, and the soft murmur of the falling waters procured a temporary alleviation. We are told, however, that for three years preceding his death, Mæcenas never slept.

PELASGI.

A name given to the most ancient inhabitants of Greece. They founded colonies in Asia Minor, the islands of the Ægean Sea, and in Italy. The

Cyclopean remains in these countries are generally attributed to the Pelasgi. These structures are remarkable for the immense size of the stones of which they are built.

PLINIUS, (Secundus C.)

A Roman writer, generally known as Pliny the Elder, is equally celebrated as a historian and a naturalist. It is not easy to understand how one man could have followed so many different avocations, filled high offices under different emperors, and yet have found time for such a vast amount of composition. While still quite young, Pliny served in Germany, where he commanded a troop of cavalry; he afterwards practised as a pleader at the Roman bar, filled the office of procurator in Spain, and we find him, at the time of his death, in command of the fleet which guarded the coast of Italy.

The application of Pliny to literary pursuits was uninterrupted. He rose to his studies at two in the morning, and during the entire day, whether in the bath, at table, or sitting in his garden, he either listened to reading, wrote, or dictated. Even on his journeys and military expeditions, a secretary always sat in his chariot. We are told that in winter Pliny was careful to provide him with a warm glove of peculiar make, that his fingers might not be too much benumbed to hold the stylus.

We have but one complete work of this author, his Natural History, in thirty-seven books. It treats, not only of natural history, properly so called, but also of astronomy, biography, history, physiology, medicine and the fine arts. The portion which treats of animals possesses now but little interest.

In many instances, the description is so vague as to leave us in doubt as to the particular animal he would designate. He also mingles facts, really observed, with fables of winged horses, monsters with human heads and the tails of scorpions, etc. The ten books on botany are open to the same objections. He attributes to many plants properties altogether fabulous, and his work, although formerly much quoted on these points, has rendered very little service to the art of medicine. The case is different where he speaks of geography, history and the fine arts. On all these points, he imparts much valuable information of which we would otherwise be deprived. The Natural History may be considered, from its wide range of subjects, a sort of Cyclopædia, and it is said that if the Latin language were lost, it might be restored from this work alone.

'Pliny perished in the great eruption of Mount Vesuvius which destroyed the towns of Herculaneum and Pompeii. He observed the phenomena accompanying it from the deck of his ship. Wishing to take a nearer view, and also to succor some of his friends whose villas lay near the scene of peril, he steered across the bay, and landed at the foot of the mountain. The next morning, while pursuing his investigations, regardless of the remonstrances of his friends, he was suffocated by the noxious vapors of the volcano. His body was discovered three days later, entirely uninjured, and in an attitude of repose.

C. PLINIUS CÆCILIUS SECUNDUS, nephew of the preceding, is generally distinguished as Pliny the Younger. Under the care of his uncle he made such rapid progress in literature, that he was generally accounted one of the most learned men of his age.

He began his career as an orator at the early age of nineteen. After filling the high offices of quæstor, consul and augur, Pliny was appointed by Trajan governor of Bithynia. It was from this country that he wrote his celebrated letter in favor of the Christians. It is interesting and important, as showing the progress of Christianity, and bearing testimony to the purity of life which was the distinguishing mark of its professors.

Pliny has left a collection of letters in ten books. They are addressed to some of the most celebrated persons of the time, and are valuable and interesting for the information they convey with regard to public events, and the manners and habits of his contemporaries. The style of these letters is studied, and they have none of the ease and familiarity of friendly correspondence. It seems probable that they were intended rather for posterity, than for the persons to whom they were ostensibly addressed.

PROCOPIUS.

One of the most celebrated historians of the Eastern Empire. He flourished during the reigns of Justin the Elder and Justinian, and accompanied Belisarius as secretary on his military expeditions.

SIMONIDES.

This poet excelled particularly in elegiac verse When the most distinguished poets of Greece wrote verses in honor of those who fell at Marathon, the elegy of Simonides took the prize, although Æschylus was one of the competitors. The compositions of the great tragedian were deficient in the tenderness and pathos for which Simonides was particularly distinguished. The lament of Danaë, and a few scattered fragments, are all that remain of his verses, but these are sufficient to prove that his reputation in this respect was well deserved.

Simonides brought the epigram to all the perfection of which it was capable. The most celebrated of his epitaphs is the monumental inscription composed for the Spartans who died at Thermopylæ: "Stranger, tell the Lacedæmonians that we lie here in obedience to their laws."

Simonides was held in high esteem at the court

of Hiero, king of Syracuse. This prince having inquired of him concerning the nature of God, the poet requested a day to deliberate on the subject. When Hiero repeated his question on the morrow, he asked for two days. As he continued in this manner, doubling the number of days, the king required an explanation. Simonides replied that he postponed his answer, because, the longer he meditated on the subject, the more obscure it became, and the more he felt his inability to treat it in an adequate manner.

Simonides was the master of Pindar; he lived to a very advanced age, so that he became the contemporary of the Pisistratidæ and of Pausanias, king of Sparta. This poet is accused of having become mercenary in his old age, and Greek writers speak of him as the first who wrote verses for money. In this connection, we have a story which would show that the poet was not believed to have forfeited the favor of the gods by his avarice.

While residing at the court of Scopas, king of Thessaly, he was engaged by that prince to compose a poem in his honor for an approaching banquet. Whether Simonides found the exploits of Scopas too barren a subject for his muse, or that his piety led him to introduce higher themes, we do not know; but when the verses were recited before the assembled court, the praises of Castor and Pollux were mingled largely with those of his royal patron.

A mortal might have been content to share his honors with the divine pair; but Scopas grudged every line which did not celebrate his own fame. When Simonides approached to receive his reward, the king gave him half the appointed sum, saying, that was for his part; for what related to Castor and Pollux, they would no doubt bestow a generous recompense. The disconcerted poet returned to his place amid the jeers and laughter of the guests. In a little while, a slave brought him word that two young men on horseback were at the gate, and desired earnestly to speak with him. Simonides went out, but found no one; while he was looking to see which way the strangers had gone, the roof of the palace fell with a terrible crash, burying Scopas and his guests beneath the ruins.

On being informed of the appearance of the young men who had sent for him—of their snow white steeds and shining armor, he knew that it was indeed Castor and Pollux who had acknowledged, in this manner, the homage of his verse.

SOPHOCLES

Was the second in order of time of the great tragic poets of Greece. In true dramatic excellence, he is generally considered the first. The poet was only sixteen when he was selected to lead the chorus of Athenian youths who celebrated with lyre and song the erection of the trophy in honor of the victory at Salamis. In his twenty-fifth year, he carried off the tragic prize from Æschylus. He gained the same triumph over other competitors, taking the first prize on twenty-four different occasions.

Irreproachable in private life, distinguished for his skill in every manly exercise, and a rare excellence in the arts of poetry and music, Sophocles was considered by his admiring countrymen as an especial favorite of the gods. The remark of the ancient sage that no man is to be accounted happy before he dies, was verified in the case of this great poet. If the morning of his life was bright in the lustre of national glory and personal renown, the evening was clouded by the misfortunes of his country, and domestic unhappiness. Sophocles served with courage, but without gaining much distinction, in the Peloponnesian war, and was a witness of the miseries which that fatal struggle brought upon Greece. He died in the year 405, B. C., a few months before the defeat of Ægos-potamos completed the misfortunes of Athens. He was deeply lamented by the Athenians, who seem to forget the calamities of the time in their grief at the loss of so illustrious a citizen. Sophocles wrote one hundred and thirty dramas, of which seven remain. Of these, the Œdipus Tyrannus and the Antigone are the most admired.

STRABO.

A celebrated geographer, born at Amasea, in Pontus, about the year 24, B. C. He spent many years in travelling, at first for his own gratification, and in the pursuit of knowledge, but afterwards by the order of Augustus. He was already advanced in life when he compiled his great work on geography. It is divided into seventeen books, and contains much valuable and interesting information with regard to the manners and customs of the nations he had visited.

Little was known at that time of the extent and form of earth. Strabo imagined that the entire habitable portion was included between two meridians, one of which passed through the island of Ierne, (Ireland,) and the other through Ceylon.

TITICACA.

A lake in Bolivia, celebrated for the ruins of Tiahuanico on its shores. They stand on an eminence which, from the water-marks surrounding it, seems to have been formerly an island in the lake. So great a change has taken place, that the level of the lake is now 135 feet lower, and its shores 12 miles distant. These ruins are believed to be the most ancient on the American continent. The Peruvians knew nothing of their origin, but had a vague tradition that they were built by giants in a single night. They regarded them, therefore, with superstitious awe, and connected them, as we have seen, with the fables of their mythology. These ruins, like some in the Old World, are often called cyclopean, on account of the size of the blocks of stone used in their construction. There are still remaining, monolithic pillars, statues and doorways, sculptured in a style entirely different from that observed on any other American monuments. We may form some idea of the size of the blocks used, from the measurement of one doorway, which is 10 ft. high, and 13 ft. broad, with an opening, 6 ft. 4 inches, by 3 ft. 2 inches, the whole being cut from a single stone.

Some of the buildings appear to have been of pyramidal form, and to have covered several acres. Of the people who executed such stupendous works, we know absolutely nothing, except that they preceded the Peruvians, and were farther advanced in the arts of civilized life than any nation existing on the continent at the time of its discovery.

VARRO

A Latin writer, celebrated for his extensive learning. He is said to have composed five hundred volumes, all of which are now lost, with the exception of two treatises; one on agriculture, the other on the Latin language. The latter is dedicated to Cicero, an intimate friend of the author.

The life of Varro was eventful : he was favored by Julius Cæsar, proscribed by Antony, and passed his later years in literary ease under the protection of Augustus. Speaking of Varro, St Augustine says, that "it is an equal subject of wonder, how one who read such a number of books, could find time to compose so many volumes; and how he who composed so many volumes, could have found leisure to peruse such a variety of books."

INDEX.

A.

Acestes, 173.
Achab, 214.
Achilles, 58, 152, 153, 166, 98.
Acœtes, 42.
Acrisius, 131
Admetus, 31.
Adonis, 53, 216.
Adrastus 168.
Æacus, 102.
Ægeus, 121, 122.
Ægisthus. 153 164.
Æneas, 171.
Æneid, 148.
Æolus, 67.
Æschylus, 170 199, 202, 291.
Æsculapius, 30, 188.
Æson, 119.
Æetes, 120
Agamedes, 184.
Agamemnon, 152.
Agathocles, 214.
Ages of the World, 18.
Agenor, 26.
Aglaia, 53.
Ajax, 141, 157.
Ahriman, 218.
Alcestis, 31.
Alcithoë, 41.
Alcibiades, 38, 193.
Alcmena, 114.
Alecto, 101.
Alexander, 187, 193.
Alfheim, 252.
Alpheus, 91.
Althea, 140.
Amazons, 135.
Ambarvalia, 79.
Amphion, 88, 128.
Amphitrite, 93.
Anchises, 171, 174
Andromache, 167, 172
Andromeda, 132.
Antigone, 169.
Antilochus, 58.
Apelles, 113, 193.
Apis, Serapis, 209, 210.
Apollo, Phœbus, 176, 26, 28 30, 33, 259, 184, 182, 152.
Arachne, 47.
Arcas, 44.
Arethusa, 91.
Argonauts, 120
Argus, 37.
Ariadne, 122.
Arion, 126.
Ascalaphus, 76.
Ascanius, 171.
Asgard, 241.
Ashtaroth, Astarte, 216.
Aske, 240.
Astræa, 80.
Astyanax, 167.
Atalanta, 52, 141.
Attalus, 73.
Athamas, 97, 119.
Atlas, 36, 129.

310 INDEX.

Atropos, 101.
Audax, Ap. Cl., 71.
Augurs, 178.
Aurora, Eos, 56.
Avatars, 222.
Avernus, 100.
Aztecs, 274.

B.

Baal, Bel, 213, 258.
Bacchanalia, 40.
Bacchantes, 41.
Bacchus, 32, 39, 122, 126, 186.
Bakoo, 219.
Baldur, 248.
Bards, 260.
Belides, 104.
Bellerophon, 104, 137.
Bellona, 35.
Belus, 213.
Belvidere, Apollo, 208.
Bifrost, 241.
Bona Dea, 73.
Bonzes, 232.
Bragi, 245.
Brahma, 221
Brennus, 84.
Briareus, 103.
Buddha, 226.

C.

Cacus, 65.
Cadmus, 26.
Caduceus, 36.
Cæculus, 65.
Cæsar, Augustus, 63, 147, 149.
Cæsar, Julius, 258, 292.
Calchas, 152, 153, 167.
Calliope, 82, 125.
Callista, 44.
Calypso, 159.
Cambyses, 59, 187.
Camul, 260.
Carnac, 272.
Cassandra, 152, 172.
Cassiopeia, 132.
Castalian fount, 189.
Castes, 225.

Cecrops, 46.
Castor, 123, **141**.
Celeus, 78.
Centaurs, 104.
Cephalus, 56.
Cepheus, 132.
Cerberus, 101, 116.
Ceres, Demeter, 17, 75, 76, **142**
Cestus, 50.
Ceyx, 138.
Charon, 100.
Charybdis, 158.
Chimæra, 104, 134.
Chione, 88
Chiron, 114.
Cholula, 280.
Cicero, 148, 293.
Cinyras. 53.
Circe, 96.
Claudia, 73.
Cleomenes, 208.
Clio, 82.
Clotho, 101.
Clymene, 33, 123.
Clytemnestra, 153, **164**.
Cœneus, 52.
Confucius, 228-9.
Consualia, 94.
Constantine, 184, 86.
Corcyreans, 181.
Coricancha, 287.
Corybantes, Galli, **73**.
Creon, 169.
Creusa, 120.
Crœsus, 183.
Cromlechs, 271.
Cupid, 50.
Cuzco, 287.
Cyane, 76.
Cybele, 72.
Cyclops, 30, 65.
Cynisca, 193.
Cyparissus, 30.

D.

Dædalus, 137.
Dagon, 217.
Danaè, 131.
Danaus, 104.

INDEX.

Daphne, 33.
Deianira, 117.
Delos, 54.
Delphi, 181.
Demosthenes, 181, 295.
Deucalion, 136.
Diana, 29, 87, 91, 152.
Dictys, 132.
Dido, 172.
Diodorus, 181, 259, 295
Diomedes, 46, 116.
Dindymus, Mt., 72.
Dionysius, 23, 194.
Dodona, 180.
Dolmens, 272.
Domitian, 70.
Druids, 258, 261.
Druidesses, 264.
Dryades, 90, 143.

E.

Echo, 91.
Eclogues, 147, 178.
Eddas, 239.
Electra, 164.
Eleusinian Mysteries, 77.
Elves, 250, 251, 252.
Elysium, 174, 104.
Embla, 241.
Ephesus, Temple of, 89
Epidaurus, 188.
Epimetheus, 124.
Erato, 82.
Erigone, 81.
Erisichthon, 143-4.
Erostratus, 89.
Esus, 258.
Eteocles, 168.
Eumenides, 102.
Euphrosyne, 53.
Euripides, 170, 193, 295
Europa, 26.
Euryale, 131.
Eurydice, 125.
Eurystheus, 114.
Euterpe. 82.

F.

Fates, 101, 140.
Fauns, 85.
Fenris, 247-8, 255.
Flora, 92.
Fo, 233.
Frey, 244.
Freya, 244.
Frigga, 248, 249.
Frost Giants, 240, 249
Furies, 101, 201.

G.

Games, Classic, 191.
Ganymede, 43.
Georgics, 148.
Genghis, Kan, 237.
Germanicus, 211.
Geryon, 104, 116.
Giants, 209.
Gnomes, 244, 252.
Gorgons, 47, 132.
Graces, 53.
Gradivus, Mars, 35.
Guatama, 226.
Guebers or Guebres, 220

H.

Hadrian, 189.
Hæmon, 106.
Halcyone, 138.
Halcyons, 139.
Hamadryades, 90.
Harpies, 104.
Harpocrates, 212.
Hebe, 118.
Hecate, 87.
Hector, 154, 166.
Hecuba, 155.
Heimdall, 245.
Hela, 245, 248, 251.
Helen, 52, 155.
Helenus, 172.
Helicon, Mt., 48, 146.
Hell, 100.

Helle, 119.
Hercules, 31, 77, 114, 191, 192, 195.
Hermione, 166.
Hermod, 249.
Herodotus, 187, 194, 296.
Hesiod, 146, 83.
Hesperides, 116, 130.
Hinnom, 215.
Hippocrene, 48.
Hippolytus, 30.
Hippomenes, 52.
Hodur, 246.
Homer, 145.
Huitzilopotchli, 275.
Hyacinthus, 30.
Hyades, 40, 130.
Hyperboreans, 182, 259.
Hyperion, 158.

I.

Ibycus, 202.
Icarus, 137, 156.
Ida, Mt., 51, 24, 171.
Iduna, 245.
Iliad, 146.
Inachus, 38.
Incas, 285.
Iphitus, 192.
Ino, 97, 119.
Io, 38, 209.
Iole, 117.
Iona, 270.
Iphigenia, 52, 165.
Iphitus, 191.
Iris, 43.
Isis, 38, 210.
Isthmian Games, 196.
Ixion, 103.
Iulus, 175.

J.

Janus, 17, 61, 63.
Japetus, 123.
Jason, 119, 141.
Jobates, 134.
Jocasta, 106.

Jotunheim
Juggerna
Juno, 25, 28, 30, 43, 51, 114, 175.
Jupiter, 17, 19, 23, 131, 159.
Jupiter Ammon, 186.
Justin, (Saint,) 178, 296.
Juvenal, 210, 212, 297.

K.

Kalki, 223.
Krishna, 223.

L.

Labyrinth, 121, 137.
Lachesis, 101.
Laius, 167.
Lama, Grand. 235-7.
Laomedon, 57.
Lao-tze, 228-231.
Lara, 108.
Lares, 108.
Latinus, 174.
Latona, 29, 54.
Lavinia, 174.
Leda, 123.
Lemnos, 64.
Lethe, 101, 104.
Lucothea, 98.
Loki, 247-250, 243, 251, 256.
Lotus eaters, 158.
Lupercus, 84.
Luxor, 59.
Lycaon, 28.
Lycomedes, 153.

M.

Mæcenas, 147, 297.
Maia, 36.
Mama Oello Huaco, 285
Manco Capac, 285.
Mania, 108.
Marathon, 81.
Mars, Ares, 34.
Marsyas, 31.
Medea, 119.
Medusa, 47, 94.

INDEX.

Megæra, 101.
Mcgalecia, 73.
Meganira, 78.
Meleager, 140.
Melicertes, 97, 196.
Melpomene, 82.
Memnon, 58.
Menelaus, 52.
Menhirs, 271.
Mentor, 146.
Mercury, Hermes, 36, 37
Mestra, 144.
Metamorphoses, 150.
Metempsychoses, 223.
Mezentius, 175.
Midas, 31.
Midgard serpent, 247.
Minerva, Pallas Athenæ, 27, 45, 51, 88, 166.
Minos, 102. 121, 142, 137.
Minotaur, 121.
Mistletoe, rite of the, 262.
Mnemosyne, 82.
Moloch, 214.
Momus, 67.
Mona, 270.
Montezuma, 283.
Muses, 48, 82.

N.

Naiades, 90.
Narcissus, 92.
Nemesis, 81.
Neptune, 17, 24, 54, 68, 93, 144.
Nereides, 90.
Nero, 184-90, 127.
Nessus, 117.
Nestor, 141.
Niffleheim, 241, 246.
Niobe, 88, 128.
Nisus, 142.
Norns, 241.
Numa, 63, 110.
Nymphs, 90.

O.

Oannes, 217.
Odin, 240-2, 245-6.

Odyssey, 146-157.
Oceanus, 87.
Oceanides, 87-90.
Œdipus, 167, 106.
Œneus, 140.
Olympiads. 192.
Olympic Games, 191.
Olympus, Mt., 18.
Ops, Rhea, 24.
Oracles, 180.
Oreades, 90.
Orestes, 164.
Orion, 131.
Ormuzd, Ormasdes, 218.
Orpheus, 96, 125.
Osiris, 38, 209.
Ouisneach, 268.
Ovid, 148.

P.

Pachacamac, 284.
Palamedes, 157.
Pales, 92.
Palæmon, 98.
Palladium, 46, 157.
Pan, 31, 84, 184.
Pandora, 124
Pariahs, 225
Paris, 51.
Parnassus, Mt., 181, 189, 136.
Parthenon, 207.
Parsees, 220.
Patroclus, 154.
Pausanias, 184.
Pegasus, 48, 135.
Pelasgi, 181, 263, 299.
Peleus, 51, 98, 141, 153.
Pelops, 103.
Penates, 108, 171.
Penelope, 156, 160.
Pentheus, 41.
Perdix, 137.
Periander, 126.
Pericles, 204.
Perseus, 47, 94, 128
Peru, 284.
Petasus, 36.
Phaeton, 33.
Phæacia, 160.

Phœnix, 107.
Phidias, 81, 206.
Philip, 193.
Philoctetes, 118.
Philomelus, 184.
Phineus, 133.
Phorcus or Proteus, 94.
Phryxus, 119.
Pierides, 83.
Pleiades, 130.
Pliny, 139, 299.
Pluto, 24, 76, 99.
Plutus, 100.
Pollux, 123, 141.
Polydectes, 132.
Polybus, 168.
Polydorus, 155.
Polyhymnia, 83.
Polyidus, 135.
Polymnestor, 155.
Polynices, 168.
Polyphemus, 65.
Polyxena, 155.
Pomona, 92.
Pou-tou, 234.
Priests, Aztec, 278.
Priestesses, Aztec, 279.
Priam, 51, 154.
Procris, 56.
Procopius, 269, 302.
Prœtus, 137.
Prometheus, 98, 123.
Proserpine, Persephone, 31, 76, 100.
Proteus, 95.
Pulcher, Cl., 179.
Pylades, 164.
Pyrrha, 136.
Pythia, 165, 181.
Pythian Games, 195.
Python, 29, 195.

Q.

Quetzalcoatl, 275.
Quirinus, Mars, 34.

R.

Ragnarok, 254.
Raymi, 289.

Rhadamanthus, 102.
Runic Letters, 258, 263.

S.

Salii, 35.
Salmoneus, 104.
Samhain, 266.
Samund Sigfüsson, 239.
Santa Sophia, 90.
Saturnalia, 62.
Saturn, 17, 24, 61.
Satyrs, 85.
Scylla, 96, 142.
Semele, 39.
Sibyls, 176.
Sibyl, Cumæan, 173, 176.
Sifa, 243.
Siguna, 252.
Silenus, 32-40.
Sirens, 95.
Sisyphus, 103, 134.
Siva, 222.
Skalds, 239.
Solymi, 135.
Sophocles, 170, 304.
Sphinx, 105.
Statues, 206.
Stonehenge, 259, 272.
Strabo, 306.
Strophius, 164.
Styx, 33, 101.
Sudras, 224.
Sylla, 158, 184, 189.
Syrinx, 85.

T.

Tantalus, 88, 103.
Tao-sse, 229.
Tara, 268.
Tarann, 260.
Tarquin, 86, 177.
Tauric festival, 258, 267.
Telamon, 141.
Telemachus, 157, 161.
Terminus, 85.
Tezcatlipoca, 281.
Terpsichore, 82.
Teutates, 259, 266.

Thalia, 53, 83.
Thammuz, 216.
Thamyris, 83.
Theatres, 197.
Themis, 80.
Theseus, 121, 141.
Thetis, 98, 153.
Thor, 242-4.
Thoth, 259.
Thrym, 242-3.
Tisiphone, 101.
Titan, 24.
Tithonus, 57.
Titicaca, 285, 306.
Tityus, 103.
Tlaloc, 281.
Toltecs, 274.
Triads, 259.
Triptolemus, 78.
Tristia, 149.
Triton, 94.
Trophonius, 184.
Tse-tse, 231.
Tuisco, 256.
Turnus, 175.
Typhon, 102, 209.

U.

Ulysses, 46, 154-156, 96.
Urania, 83.

V.

Valhalla, 242.
Valkyrior, 247.
Varro, 176, 307.
Ve, 240.
Vedas, 221.
Venus, 49, 51, 53, 65. 171
Vertumnus, 86.
Vesta, 69.
Vestal Virgins, 70.
Vidar, 246.
Vili, 240.
Viracocha, 284.
Virgil, 147.
Virgins of the Sun,
Virginia, 111.
Virtues personified, 110.
Vishnu, 222.
Vulcan, Hephæstus, 19, 64,
  68, 154.
Vulcania, 65.
Vyassa, 221.

X.

Xerxes, 183.

Y.

Ymir, 240.

Z.

Zend-avesta, 218.
Zenodorus, 260.
Zoroaster, 218.

THE END.

www.ingramcontent.com/pod-product-compliance
Lightning Source LLC
Chambersburg PA
CBHW022045230426
43672CB00008B/1076